TO MY SON STEVEN,
HOPE YOU EJOY THE BOOK!
LOVE YOU,
DAD...

NO WAY OUT

NO WAY OUT

THE UNTOLD STORY OF THE B-24 "LADY BE GOOD" AND HER CREWS

STEVEN R. WHITBY

Copyright © 2020 by Steven R. Whitby

Library of Congress Control Number: 2020930864

All rights reserved. No part of this work may be reproduced or used in any form or by any means—graphic, electronic, or mechanical, including photocopying or information storage and retrieval systems—without written permission from the publisher.

The scanning, uploading, and distribution of this book or any part thereof via the Internet or any other means without the permission of the publisher is illegal and punishable by law. Please purchase only authorized editions and do not participate in or encourage the electronic piracy of copyrighted materials.

"Schiffer Military" and the arrow logo are trademarks of Schiffer Publishing, Ltd.

Designed by Justin Watkinson
Cover design by Ashley Millhouse
Type set in Abolition / Minion Pro / Univers LT Std

ISBN: 978-0-7643-6037-4
Printed in China

Published by Schiffer Publishing, Ltd.
4880 Lower Valley Road
Atglen, PA 19310
Phone: (610) 593-1777; Fax: (610) 593-2002
E-mail: Info@schifferbooks.com
Web: www.schifferbooks.com

For our complete selection of fine books on this and related subjects, please visit our website at www.schifferbooks.com. You may also write for a free catalog.

Schiffer Publishing's titles are available at special discounts for bulk purchases for sales promotions or premiums. Special editions, including personalized covers, corporate imprints, and excerpts, can be created in large quantities for special needs. For more information, contact the publisher.

We are always looking for people to write books on new and related subjects. If you have an idea for a book, please contact us at proposals@schifferbooks.com.

DEDICATION

To the nine gallant men this story revolves around, who gave their last full measure against all the odds of survival, but in the end, they had no way out:

William J. Hatton

Robert F. Toner

Dp Hays

John S. Woravka

Harold J. Ripslinger

Robert E. LaMotte

Guy E. Shelley

Vernon L. Moore

Samuel E. Adams

CONTENTS

	✪ FOREWORD	7
	✪ INTRODUCTION	8
	✪ ACKNOWLEDGMENTS	9
CHAPTER 1	✪ GENESIS	10
CHAPTER 2	✪ LT. ROSE'S CREW	16
CHAPTER 3	✪ LT. HATTON'S CREW	36
CHAPTER 4	✪ THE MISSION	46
CHAPTER 5	✪ BAILOUT	54
CHAPTER 6	✪ THE DISCOVERY	60
CHAPTER 7	✪ THE FIRST USAF / US ARMY FLIGHT TO THE CRASH SITE	80
CHAPTER 8	✪ THE INSPECTION	90
CHAPTER 9	✪ THE SEARCH FOR THE CREW	130
CHAPTER 10	✪ THE DISCOVERY OF FIVE CREW REMAINS	162
CHAPTER 11	✪ SEARCH FOR THE FINAL FOUR: OPERATION CLIMAX	188
CHAPTER 12	✪ MYSTERIES AND THE SO-CALLED CURSE OF THE LADY BE GOOD	248
	✪ INDEX	255

FOREWORD

By the age of twelve, I had become an avid reader of newspapers. I would search out anything to do with aviation, since by that point in my life I was completely fascinated with aircraft, and especially those of the World War II generation. Therefore, I was captivated by an item in the *Fort Worth Star-Telegram* headlined something like "Mystery Bomber Found in the Desert." That was, of course, the beginning of the Lady Be Good saga.

At that time, my father was with the first Convair B-58 Hustler unit, preparing to go operational with the USAF, and many of the personnel involved were World War II veterans, so I would often hear great first-person stories of that conflict. Learning of my interest, some veterans gave me aeronautical bits and pieces they had gathered over the years. One such item was a nose art panel cut from a damaged Liberator—a B-24 that operated from the same base as Lady Be Good. My interest in the B-24 and other World War II aircraft led to a flying trip arranged by my father to Tulsa, Oklahoma, where the sad hulk of a B-24J rested on its tail. I climbed through the bomber—the first time I had been in a World War II aircraft—and imagined what it was like for the crew of the Lady in those cramped spaces. By that point, newspaper and magazine articles abounded on the fate of the aircraft and its crew, and I cut those out and saved them.

Time, as always, moves forward, yet for those of us involved in aviation and aviation history, the saga of Lady Be Good and its heroic crew always remained fresh. A few relics were returned to the USAF Museum, but the majority of the bomber was simply abandoned to the desert. This was long before today's intense interest in aviation preservation—an interest that probably would have resulted in the return of Lady Be Good to America.

As the years passed, there would be many articles and at least one book and a television movie on the fate of this single bomber. I would become intimately involved with the operation of restored World War II aircraft and eventually became the owner of Challenge Publications, whose magazines center on aviation and nautical history. It was through these magazines that I would meet Steve Whitby and would find a kindred spirit in preserving the momentous events of the Second World War.

Among his many interests, Steve has an abiding passion for the story of Lady Be Good, and I must admit I was rather stunned by his dedication in finding and recording the minutest details of that bomber and its men. I was also most impressed by the number of photographs he had gathered. We often discussed that all this material must be put into a book to record the tale of the Lady for future generations. The result of Steve's decades of dedicated research is now before you, the reader. As noted, there has been much written about Lady Be Good, but you will not find anything better than this intense and passionate recording of an intriguing slice of American history.

Michael O'Leary
Publisher / Editor: Air Classics Magazine, Warbirds International,
Mustangs International, and Sea Classics
May 21, 2020
Calabasas, California

INTRODUCTION

In 1959, as an eleven-year-old boy fascinated with flying, reading books on World War II, and growing up on stories from my father, who served aboard an aircraft carrier in the Pacific (USS *Hornet*) launching airstrikes against the Japanese, as well as stories that my mother related to me concerning what her first cousin did during the war, flying B-24 Liberators from his base in England and bombing targets in Germany, you can imagine my excitement and amazement at that age when news was flashed around the world of the discovery of an American World War II four-engine bomber found deep in the middle of the Sahara Desert in the North African country of Libya.

That was my first glimpse into the mystery surrounding this aircraft and her crew. Then the March 7, 1960, *Life* magazine article came out, with photos. I ended up with a copy and drank it up; this was when the mystery was still unsolved. Fast forward almost sixty years; my interest in this never faded, but with everything life throws at you, until a few years back I was never able to really pursue a driving interest I had in this.

What really started me on the road to writing this book was a 1:48-scale model diorama I built of the Lady Be Good back in 1982, then donated it to the March Air Force Base Museum here in Southern California. Jim Walker saw a photo of the model a few years later in some publication and contacted me. It turned out he was going to be writing a book on the 376th Bomb Group and thought I had a talent for detail on this type of aircraft. After that, a lifelong friendship was struck, and a few years later I did several pieces of graphic artwork on B-24s for his book, as well as some charts and graphs. Jim was going to write this book but died in the hospital during surgery. Before he passed away, he had put me in contact with a good friend of his, Wesley A. Neep, who was a forensic-identification specialist working for the US Army since before the end of World War II.

In 1959, Wes headed the US Army and Air Force team that went into the Libyan Desert right after the discovery of the plane, to find out what happened to the crew. I became good friends with Wes, who helped me piece this story together. Over the next few years, I flew up to Seattle for interviews with Wes and will forever be grateful for all his help. Wes passed away at the age of ninety-four not long after my last visit with him. These two men, Wes and Jim, above all else; without their help with information and photographs, none of this would have been possible. Rest in peace, my friends.

ACKNOWLEDGMENTS

I'm the author of note for this publication, but these people should also be listed because this book could never have been written without their help. I'd like to thank or acknowledge the people who contributed or helped me in bringing this book to reality.

Wesley A. Neep, who supplied me with a wealth of information and never-before-published photographs, slides, and negatives, and who was the one who led the search party looking for the crew of Lady Be Good in 1959–60. Wes's insight into what it was like to be one of the first people to lay eyes on this plane in 1959, and the subsequent search for her crew over the next year and a half after the plane's discovery, was greatly appreciated. RIP, Wes.

James W. Walker was going to write this story, but sadly he passed away during surgery before that ever happened. Jim's diligent work on digging up obscure information on this subject was greatly appreciated, RIP, Jim.

Dawson (Doc) Rose, Lady Be Good's first pilot, who with his crew flew her across the Atlantic to North Africa but, by a quirk of fate, never saw her again a few days after their arrival at their base. RIP, Dawson.

Sheldon (Shelley) McConnell, who flew the first USAF C-130A out to the crash site in 1959 with two H-23 search helicopters. He supplied me with photos he took, as well as components from Lady Be Good. RIP, Shelley.

Don Venturini gave me the photographs he took out at the crash site just a week after the first investigation crew were there in order to recover the L-19 fuselage.

Casey Arnold supplied me with some of Jim Walker's slides after Jim's death.

Brandon Bonneville worked with me early on during my research.

Roger Landery supplied me with his photos from his US Army excursion out to the Lady Be Good crash site in 1962.

Michael Savvides supplied me with the photos he took at the Lady Be Good crash site during his oil exploration for BP in 1977.

Jay Arnold supplied me with photos he took at the crash site in late 1968 and 1972.

Don Poirier supplied me with the information on the SC-47's loss.

Tony John supplied me with the information on the loss of the US Army Otter.

Joseph Sites Jr.

Ed Truthan supplied the map on page 59.

CHAPTER 1 ★ GENESIS

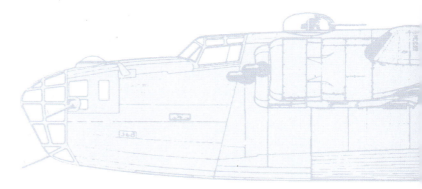

The story begins at the time of the plane's construction. It started out on paper as a Model 32 Liberator, or LB-30 cargo version of the B-24, under the provisions of the First Defense Aid "E" program to Great Britain on March 18, 1941, nine months prior to the United States entering World War II. The Lend-Lease order was for an aircraft slated for the British Royal Air Force to haul war cargo for England. But on May 12, 1941, this aircraft, along with the entire order of 629, was diverted and taken over by the United States Army Air Force, because it was thought in Washington, DC, that in a very short time, the US might be involved in the conflict in Europe.

These 629 aircraft all were assigned US Army Air Force designations, or serial numbers, and again, only on paper, changed from the Lend-Lease cargo version to the four-engine bomber type. Thus, B-24D-25-CO, serial number 41-24301, the 24,301st aircraft ordered by the US government, came into existence.

Construction started in the winter of 1941 in San Diego, California, at the Consolidated Aircraft Factory, making slow progress until Pearl Harbor was bombed in December. After the US entered the war, everything changed, but smooth, fast war production hadn't really kicked in yet.

Modifications to this production block of "D" models were integrated into the assembly line through 1942, until 41-24301 was finally rolled out into the bright, Southern California sunshine reflecting off her fresh olive-drab-and gray factory paint job. The first test flight out over San Diego County and the Pacific was made on December 4. Shortly after this, on December 8, she was officially accepted into the US Army Air Force.

Early in 1942, she was picked up at Lindberg Field in San Diego by two Wasps (Women's Air Force Service Pilots) and flown to Fort Worth, Texas, for modifications that would fit the theater of operations she would eventually be assigned to. One of the modifications done at Fort Worth was a complete repaint from her olive drab to a bright "desert pink," indicating she would be assigned to a desert theater. This particular model also had its belly or "ball" turret removed and the hole fared over with plywood.

She sat on the ramp at Fort Worth for only a few days before two more Wasps climbed aboard, fired up the four Pratt & Whitney engines, taxied out to the runway, and lifted off to fly her to the next destination, Topeka, Kansas, where bomber crews were being assembled to be pared up with new aircraft to fly off to combat zones.

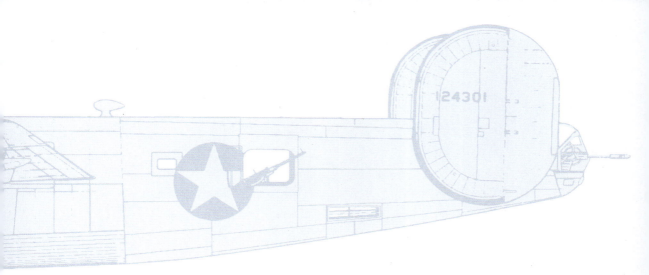

SPECIFICATIONS	CONSOLIDATED B-24D-25-CO SERIAL NUMBER 41-24301 "LADY BE GOOD"
MANUFACTURED IN SAN DIEGO, CALIFORNIA, NOVEMBER 1942	
WINGSPAN	110 ft.
LENGTH	66 ft., 4 in.
HEIGHT	18 ft.
EMPTY WEIGHT	32,505 lbs.
MAXIMUM WEIGHT	60,000 lbs.
POWER PLANT	4× Pratt & Whitney R-1830-43 twin-row engines, rated at 1,200 hp each
MAXIMUM SPEED	303 mph
MAXIMUM ALTITUDE	32,000 ft.
MAXIMUM RANGE	3,000 miles
ARMAMENT	10× Browning M2 .50-caliber machine guns
CREW	4 officers 5 enlisted

A portion of the right-side forward section of a B-24 fuselage being assembled at the Consolidated Aircraft Factory plant in San Diego, California, on February 7, 1942.

Rear fuselage sections prior to being assembled at the Consolidated plant in San Diego, California, on February 7, 1942.

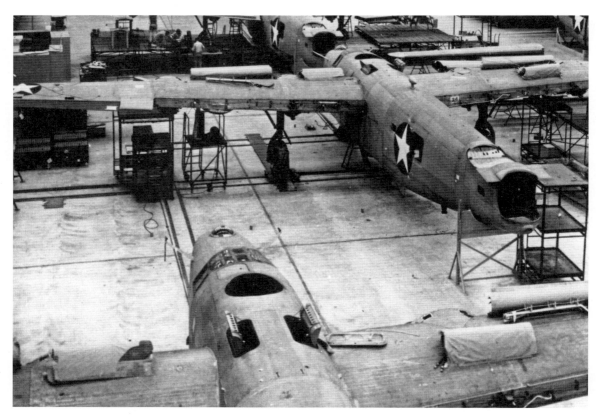

B-24D-25-CO assembly line at the Consolidated Aircraft Factory in San Diego, California. Note that the US national insignia has already been applied prior to the aircraft receiving its first coat of olive drab paint.

US Army Air Force modification center at Fort Worth, Texas, makes changes to combat aircraft prior to deployment to various war theaters. This photo was taken on February 4, 1943, and shows an olive drab B-24D-25-CO, exactly like Lady Be Good, prior to her repaint to desert pink. A P-47 and P-38 are also going through modifications in the background. Note the three .50-caliber nose gun barrels wrapped in paper for protection while being shipped.

A B-24D-25-CO having its factory olive drab paint being overpainted with desert pink after arrival at the Consolidated Modification Center, Fort Worth, Texas, early in 1943.

Cramped nose of a new B-24D, showing (*from left to right*) bombardier's toggle switch panel, ammo belt for the left-cheek .50-caliber machine gun, bomb release handles, Norden bombsight (*covered*), chin .50-caliber machine gun (*bottom center*), ammo belt for right .50-caliber machine gun, heating tube, right .50-caliber machine gun, and navigator's table.

Engineer / top turret gunner standing behind the pilot and copilot in the B-24D cockpit.

MARTIN A3 TWIN 50 CAL.
ELECTRICALLY OPERATED
DORSAL TURRET

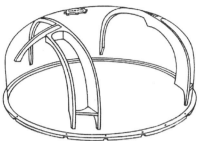

MARTIN ONE PIECE
REINFORCED PLEXIGLASS
DORSAL TURRET DOME

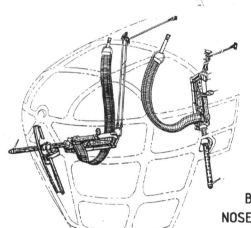

BROWNING M2 50 CAL.
HAND HELD MACHINE GUN

B-24D 50 CAL.
NOSE GUN PLACEMENT
WITH AMMO BELTS

CONSOLIDATED A6A
TWIN 50 CAL.
ELECTRICALLY OPERATED
TAIL TURRET
WITH FLASH SUPPRESSORS

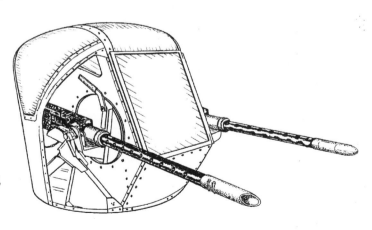

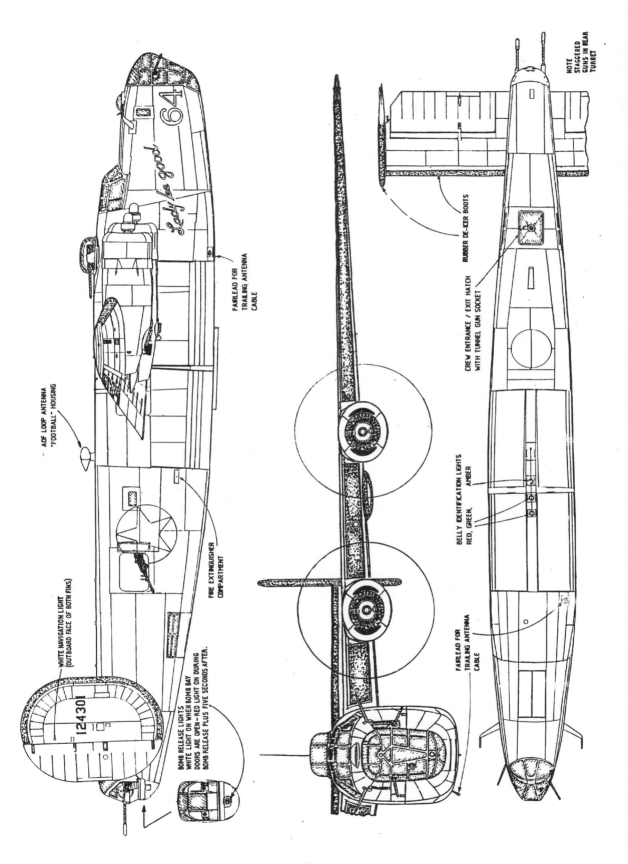

CHAPTER 2 ★ LT. ROSE'S CREW

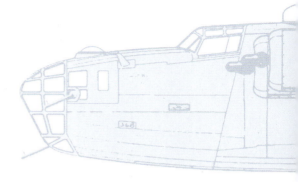

Second Lt. Samuel Dawson Rose, United States Army Air Force, or "Doc" as he was nicknamed, along with his nine-man crew—copilot, 2Lt. Ralph O. Grace; navigator, 2Lt. Millard B. Kessler; bombardier, 2Lt. Charles H. Midgley; flight engineer / top turret gunner, TSgt. William S. Nelson; tail turret gunner, SSgt. Roscoe S. Hoover; radio operator, Pvt. Carl L. Valentine; asst. engineer, Pvt. Joseph E. Maleski; left waist gunner, SSgt. Allyn Leavy; and right waist gunner, SSgt. Charles Marshall—had arrived in Topeka, Kansas, on January 5, 1943, for further flight training in B-24s prior to assignment in a combat zone. Toward the end of the month, Doc and his crew heard that six brand-new B-24Ds were slated to be ferried into Topeka by Wasps from the modification center at Fort Worth. These were to be issued to six of the crews in Topeka and would be the aircraft they would be taking overseas.

This modification center made changes to the aircraft to fit the theater of operations they would be sent to. At that time, they had no idea where they would be assigned: the Pacific, China-Burma-India, Europe, the Aleutian Islands, or North Africa. After Sam and his crew were assigned one of these aircraft, Lt. Rose asked one of the ground crew chiefs to go down to the flight line and check to see what color 41-24301 was. He returned a short time later and said, "Pink, lieutenant." That meant Africa! Doc smiled at that. He didn't want to go to England and fly in the rain and fog, or the ice and cold in the Aleutians.

The next morning, Lt. Rose and crew went down to the flight line to take their new aircraft up for their first familiarization flight. Each crewman checked out his respective positions, finding everything brand new and in perfect working order. Sam wanted to see how she would handle at altitude, so he decided to take her up as high as her service ceiling permitted, 33,000 feet. When they reached 31,500 feet, all four Pratt & Whitney engines cut out. Lt. Rose dropped down to a lower altitude, where they got the engines restarted and went straight back to the field at Topeka. The ground crews found that the spark plug wires were shorting out across their insulation at high altitude. They immediately replaced all the plug wires on all four engines with upgraded plug wires. Other than that "minor" problem, everything else seemed to function as it should, with little or no squawks. The rest of the month, 41-24301 and her new crew were busy honing their skills with missions over the bombing range at Pueblo, Colorado. Sometime in that period, they decided to give their new aircraft a name.

One of the enlisted men on the crew (unknown which one) suggested the title to a song and movie that was popular at the time, "Lady Be Good." After a short discussion among everyone, they all agreed that sounded pretty good. Lt. Rose asked

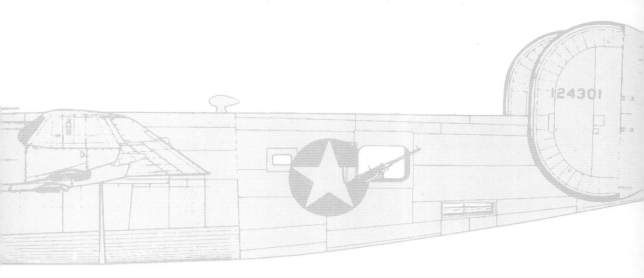

one of the ground crew to find some paint. The sergeant came back with some paint, but it was yellow, since that was all he could find on short notice. He also found someone who could paint text and apply the name in stylized letters approximately 9 inches high, at a 45-degree angle on the right side of the nose, starting down near the gray/pink demarcation line behind the cockpit and going up toward the pitot tube. The yellow paint didn't show much contrast against the pink background, but at least the plane had a name!

The morning of March 8 found the crews of all six new B-24s cleaning the snow off their planes from the winter storm the night before. They had finally been issued orders for their flight overseas, with the first leg being Morrison Field, West Palm Beach, Florida. The Lady was the last to take off and arrived in the area during a thunderstorm, so they set down at Hendricks Field, some miles away. The next morning they flew on to Morrison. When the crew departed the plane, they discovered everybody in shorts, while they were wearing high-altitude sheepskin flying suits and boots!

The next leg was a midnight takeoff for Waller Army Air Base on the island of Trinidad. After landing, base operations wanted Rose to taxi over and park among the trees, so Doc had a man sitting on each wing to help out in the parking; it didn't help. While swinging around to come to a stop, he clipped one of the wingtips on a palm tree trunk. The damage wasn't bad enough for them to repair it there, but before the base personnel could make that determination the next morning, the other five aircraft had taken off for the next leg, Belem Brazil. The Lady and her crew left the following morning, on the twelfth, for Belem, which is near the mouth of the Amazon River; here they caught up with the other five B-24s.

While in Belem, Lt. Rose took a taxi around town that night and discovered that if you honk your horn but run over somebody, you're in the clear, so everybody drove with one hand on the wheel and the other on the horn. There were no crosswalks, and everyone crossed anywhere they wanted.

The next morning, all six aircraft took off for Natal, Brazil, on the far eastern coast. Natal had no appeal, nothing but open dirt and mud on the fringes of a jungle. The ground crews fueled up the planes by hand from 5-gallon cans, which took a very long time. They had to strain the fuel through chamois to filter out the dirt.

Early the next morning, on March 14, they all took off for their ten-and-a-half-hour flight across the Atlantic to Ascension Island. Navigation was performed with the B-24 ADF (automatic directional finder) loop antenna. This unit's exterior shape is like a tapered football and is located midway atop the fuselage. Ascension Island sent out a signal that the B-24's ADF could home in on; it worked perfectly, since they all arrived safely. The ADF system would figure prominently later in the Lady Be Good's fate.

The next leg of their journey was a nine-hour flight up to Accra, on the Gold Coast of West Africa, where their aircraft were washed by the local youth, then they were refueled and off again for Khartoum. Only three hours into the flight, the Lady Be Good ran into a terrible storm that forced Lt. Rose to land at the nearest field, an RAF base at Ikeja, Nigeria.

After an overnight stay, they had an early five-and-a-half-hour flight to Maiduguri, Nigeria. This flat, desolate area was only a short stay for refueling, then on to Khartoum to be reunited with the rest of the flight, which had pushed on through the storm and landed safely. Cairo was the second-to-the-last stop before flying on to Libya, where their base of operations was located.

As the flight approached Cairo, they saw another huge dust storm over the city and surrounding area. The Lady Be Good flew into the storm, entering the landing pattern with two B-25s and a C-47. Heliopolis Airport was a British air base used for major repairs on their aircraft as well as US Army Air Force aircraft. You had to line up perfectly with the main runway or you would hit any one of the multitude of British and American Aircraft parked on either side of the runway.

Turns out the two B-25s were very short on fuel, so they had priority in landing. One of the B-25s lost power when it ran out of gas on final and crashed in the rock quarry near the field. The other B-25 and the C-47 made successful landings, with Lt. Rose landing last.

On March 25, they flew on to their new assignment as a replacement aircraft and crew for the 376th Bomb Group, located at Soluch, Libya, two days later to move to a paved runway at Berka 2 on the coast.

There wasn't much at Soluch, just tents for the personnel pitched on the sand, with some having wooden floors and a dirt runway to fly from. The control tower was a trailer and a generator parked off the runway, about midpoint, and a beacon that was a pyramid of lights about 8 feet tall; very primitive conditions. The dirt runway caused a myriad of mechanical problems with the aircraft. During landings and takeoffs, you could see the dust cloud for over 20 miles. The dirt and dust got into everything, especially the aircraft engines. When the base was first opened, they tried to use B-17s, but because the air intakes were in the leading edge of the wings, the dirt they ingested ate the engines up in one or two missions. B-24s had their intakes up on either side of the engine cowlings, much higher off the ground than B-17s. B-24 engines would last longer but still had to be replaced much sooner than normal maintenance would require.

Rose and his crew were assigned to the 376th Bomb Group, 514th Bomb Squadron. Their bomb group commander was Capt. Hal Simmons (Capt. Norm Appold later took over this position), and their group squadron commander was Col. Keith Compton, who was considered the "old man" at twenty-eight years old. Rose and his crew were ready for their first combat mission, but their aircraft wasn't.

Base operations had Lt. Rose take the Lady up for a two-hour test flight in the local area in order to complete a full list of squawks that needed to be addressed after the long flight from Topeka across the Atlantic to their base at Soluch.

Rose and his flight engineer, Sgt. Bill Nelson, came up with a list of things that needed to be addressed before their aircraft could be signed off for combat. Along with the repair of the wingtip that was damaged back at Waller Field in Trinidad, there were leaks in the oxygen and hydraulic systems, and the automatic flight control system stopped working after crossing the Atlantic. Unbeknown to Lt. Rose, that would be the last time he ever flew his aircraft. On March 31, Capt. Appold took 41-24301 up for a test flight after having most of the previous problems corrected. His goal was to sign the aircraft off as ready for combat, but he found some new discrepancies that needed to be addressed. By April 3, Lady Be Good had all of her problems corrected and was assigned to the 514th Squadron. The number "64" was painted in white on either side of the lower nose—she was ready for her first combat mission.

While the Lady Be Good was being repaired by the base mechanics, Sam and his crew were assigned to the base "clunker" for their first combat mission on April 2, 1943. There was an unofficial rule concerning brand-new replacement crews flying the worst plane in the squadron on their first mission.

Their mission was to bomb the docks at Palermo, Sicily, but because the "assigned aircraft" they drew was old, beat up, and battle scarred, and needing constant repairs, they had trouble keeping up with the rest of the squadron and lagged farther and farther behind after two of their worn engines kept cutting out. Not being able to stay with the rest of the squadron, Lt. Rose decided to divert to the British base on the island of Malta for repairs.

The base was socked in during a pounding rainstorm, but Lt. Rose made a safe landing on the short runway. The next morning, April 4, the engines on the old B-24 were repaired enough so they could return to their base at Soluch. They had an uneventful flight back, arriving at their base around 1300. After landing and securing the old B-24, they paused on their way to operations for their debriefing in order to watch their squadron take off for a late-afternoon mission to destroy the docks and shipping at Naples Harbor. To their surprise, one of the B-24s taking off for this mission was 41-24301.

Apparently, their new B-24 had passed all necessary repairs and was assigned to another crew for this particular mission. Dawson Rose and his men never saw the Lady Be Good again.

Lt. Rose and his crew went on to have some harrowing experiences up to and including their last mission over Bari, Italy, after being hit by flak over the target and bailing out of their stricken Liberator at 20,000 feet. But that's another story.

Brand-new 41-24301 on the ramp at Fort Worth, Texas, after her repaint from olive drab to desert pink, and desert modifications, February 17, 1943.

2Lt. Dawson "Doc" Rose.

Lt. Rose's crew and 41-24301 at Topeka, Kansas.

One of the six B-24Ds at Natal, Brazil, with its left main gear stuck in the mud. She was pulled out with no damage prior to her scheduled takeoff for Ascension Island.

Lt. Rose next to the Lady Be Good at Natal, Brazil. Note the handwritten "368" shipping number, applied at Fort Worth, Texas.

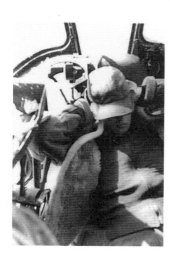

Lt. Kesler catching some sleep in the cramped nose on the journey to North Africa.

In Lady Be Good's nose, Lieutenants Kesler and Midgley plot a course across the Atlantic Ocean to Ascension Island.

Sgt. Bill Nelson, Lady Be Good's engineer, and Lieutenants Doc Rose and Ralph Grace go over fuel consumption for the four Pratt & Whitney engines on the flight across the Atlantic.

Midgley, Rose, and Grace in Cairo, Egypt, March 20, 1943.

Ground crew attempt to cover equipment near Capt. Norm Appold's B-24D G.I. Ginnie #74, as a dust storm approaches their base in Libya.

New crews assemble their quarters in the primitive conditions at Berka 2, Soluch, Libya.

Ground crews were constantly changing the Pratt & Whitney R-1320 engines because of the damage caused by dust storms.

B-24 crews load their gear into a truck after returning from an early-morning bombing mission to southern Italy.

Cannibalizing parts from damaged B-24s was common in order to keep the rest flying.

Ground crews were also very adept at reskinning damaged aircraft with new aluminum in the field.

Left and right waist gunners in a North African–based B-24D. This is looking forward toward the bomb bay.

Outdoor briefing for a mission during a sandstorm.

376th B-24Ds line up for a staggered takeoff at Soluch. After the first one took off, the rest had to contend with all the dust stirred up by the first aircraft's engines; each plane after made it worse for the next.

The blistering heat in Libya sometimes warranted a shirtless takeoff by the flight crew, later to layer up with clothing as they gained altitude.

Crew of Black Jack go over the day's mission map prior to takeoff.

CHAPTER 3 ★ LT. HATTON'S CREW

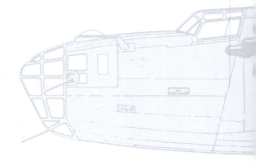

Lt. Bill Hatton, from Whitestone, New York, joined the 244th Coast Artillery Regiment, a New York Army National Guard unit, in 1940, after graduating from college in 1939. The 244th was called up in September 1940, following the attack on Pearl Harbor. Hatton applied to the Army Air Force but was at the age limit for a pilot, at twenty-four years old.

Hatton graduated from the Advanced Flying Course as a second lieutenant in July 1942. He applied as a fighter pilot, but the Army Air Force decided he was better suited for bombers and sent him to Hendricks Field, Sebring, Florida, for training in four-engine B-17s. During the first week of September, he married Amelia (Millie) Jansky near his base in Florida.

Bill turned out to be very adept at flying the B-17 and was given an aircraft commander's rating after completing the course. In October, he was sent to Davis-Monthan Field, Tucson, Arizona, for transition to the B-24, then on to New Mexico.

At Alamogordo Army Air Base, New Mexico, Lt. Hatton was matched up with his crew. Lt. Robert F. Toner was assigned to Hatton as his copilot. Toner, from Rhode Island, was a year older than Hatton at twenty-seven, an age that was considered old for a frontline combat pilot at the time. Bob applied for training as an aviation cadet in 1941 but didn't have the minimum required two-year college degree and was turned down, so he decided to go to Canada, where the academic requirements were less stringent for the Royal Canadian Air Force. The RCAF had an accelerated aircrew training program because of the need for Britain's Royal Air Force, which was then at war with both Germany and Italy. After his graduation as a RCAF pilot officer, Bob reapplied to the Army Air Force for aviation cadet training and was accepted in the wake of the mobilization after Pearl Harbor was bombed on December 7, 1941. Toner was sent to Davis-Monthan and trained in B-24s with Bill Hatton.

Lt. Dp Hays, navigator, was from Kansas City, Kansas (his first name was a composite of the first letters of his father's first and middle names, David Peter). He graduated as a second lieutenant and moved on to Alamogordo for combat crew training in November 1942. His age was twenty-three in 1943, and he was the shortest member of the crew at 5 foot 6, and weighing 125 pounds.

Lt. John S. Woravka, bombardier, was from Cleveland, Ohio, and was sent to Albuquerque, New Mexico, for bombardier training, then assigned to Hatton's crew. At twenty-six, he fit in very well with the older crew members.

Sgt. Harold J. Ripslinger, from Saginaw, Michigan, was twenty-two years old in 1943 and was assigned as the top turret gunner / flight engineer for Hatton's crew

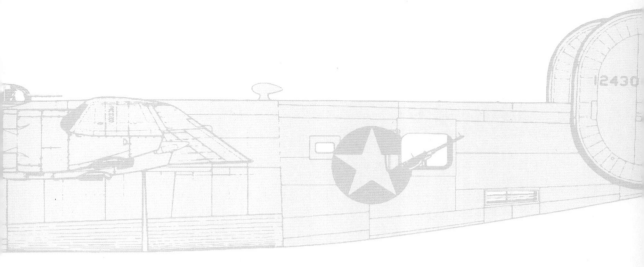

in November 1942. He was engaged when he joined the Army Air Force and was the ranking enlisted member, with the grade of technical sergeant.

Sgt. Robert F. LaMotte, also twenty-two years old, was from Lake Linden, Michigan, and was trained as a radio operator. He joined Bill Hatton's crew in training at Alamogordo.

Assistant engineer / gunner Guy E. Shelly Jr. was Hatton's age, twenty-six, in 1943 and was from New Cumberland, Pennsylvania. He was a qualified waist gunner and became Ripslinger's top turret backup on Hatton's crew.

Waist gunner Vernon L. Moore was twenty-one years old in 1943 and was from New Boston, Ohio. Moore entered the Army Air Force in March 1942 and graduated with Harold Ripslinger from the same gunnery school at Las Vegas, Nevada. They were both glad they ended up on the same crew after arriving at Alamogordo, New Mexico.

Tail gunner Sgt. Samuel E. Adams was twenty-four years old in 1943 and was from Speedwell, Kentucky. In 1941, he married Dorothy Sherman, and he was the only crew member to have a child, a son, Michael, who was born several months after Adams entered the air force. Adams was 5 foot 7 and trained as an aerial gunner with future crewmates Harold Ripslinger and Vernon Moore at Las Vegas Gunnery School. He too was glad to be with friends on the same crew at Alamogordo.

So, Hatton's crew had one twenty-seven-year-old, three twenty-six-year-olds, one twenty-four-year-old, one twenty-three-year-old, two twenty-two-year-olds, and one twenty-one-year-old by the time they came together as a crew in 1943; by far, the extreme upper end of the age limit for combat. The difference in flight time between copilot Bob Toner and pilot Bill Hatton didn't seem to be a problem between the two men. Toner had almost twice the flight time as Hatton. Bob was a bit disappointed and indicated this in letters to his family that he had not made the list of first pilots, but he accepted his assignment as copilot without any problems. On February 20, 1943, Lt. Bill Hatton and his crew took possession of a brand-new dune-tan-and-gray B-24D-30-CO, serial number 42-40081, and named it Zip. They made two shakedown flights on the twenty-first and twenty-second. During these flights, each crew member checked out the operation of every system that applied to their particular responsibility in the plane.

At the end of February, six of the crews in training at Topeka were ordered to fly their planes to Morrison Field, Florida. The first pilots included Lieutenants William Hatton and Jack Goehry. They arrived on February 27 and were at Morrison for only five days.

During a short visit to Miami, Bob Toner bought a small diary to record his combat experiences. Toner's first diary entry recorded that "All of the group departed on March 2nd for Borenquen Field, Puerto Rico." Their orders directed them to proceed via the South Atlantic route to Cairo, Egypt.

After a two-day stay at Borenquen, the four planes departed for Georgetown, Guyana. After landing at Georgetown, the bomber crews witnessed the crash of a Douglas A-20 Havoc twin engine bomber attempting to land in the poor visibility. The five-man crew were all killed in the crash.

Halfway to Natal, after flying on instruments for six hours, the weather deteriorated to the extent that they were forced to divert to Belem, Brazil. The field at Belem was out of fuel, so yet another delay was encountered until a tanker arrived with a full cargo of aviation fuel. While there, the crew preformed some needed repairs on Zip.

Dp Hays's navigation on the long flight across the Atlantic to Ascension Island was spot on when they turned into the landing pattern within two minutes of their estimated time of arrival. After arriving at Accra, West Africa, the next leg of the flight, the crew made a fifty-hour inspection on their plane.

On the route across Africa to Khartoum on March 15, after a scenic flight north along the Nile River, the crew touched down at Heliopolis Field, Cairo, Egypt, ending their twelve-day journey.

After a night in Cairo, Hatton reported to 9th Air Force headquarters and was ordered to leave that day for assignment to the 376th at Soluch, Libya. Harold Ripslinger recorded this in his diary: "Took off for Soluch at 11:30 am and landed at 2:05 pm. Flew over wreckage of Rommel's retreat, tanks and planes galore."

On March 16, 1943, they arrived at their new base at Soluch, Libya. Bill Hatton and his crew joined other replacements at Soluch, where the 376th Bomb Group was being brought up to their full complement of combat crews. Hatton reported to Capt. Hal Simmons, commander of the 514th Squadron. Tents were issued, and Zip's four officers, Hatton, Hayes, Toner, and Woravka, set up their tent next to Lt. Rose and his three officers.

For the first week after their arrival at Soluch, all new crews were lectured on the air defense corridors along the Libyan coast.

During the night of March 18, a very rare storm moved into the area, with a torrential downpour of rain lasting more than two hours flooding all the tents at Soluch and causing damage to the flight crews' personal possessions.

During a visit to the flight line on March 21 to check on their plane, Hatton and his crew found Zip missing. The B-24 they had flown all the way from Topeka to Soluch had been transferred to the 98th Bomb Group—a big disappointment, knowing now that they would not get to fly their plane in combat.

On April 2, Hatton and Bob Toner logged their first combat time during a mission to Palermo, Sicily. Hatton flew as copilot for a flight school classmate, Dick Hurd, while Bob Toner filled in for Bill McCain's regular copilot; both returned from the mission safely.

At this time, Lt. Rose's plane was still undergoing preparation for her first mission, but by the fourth, the Lady Be Good had been signed off and ready for combat. Because Lt. Rose and his crew were stuck in Malta, and Lt. Hatton and his crew had no aircraft, Capt. Simmons paired Bill Hatton and his crew with the now-operational Lady Be Good for the Naples mission.

Left to right: Lt. Bill Hatton, pilot; Lt. Robert Toner, copilot; Lt. Dp Hays, navigator; Lt. John Woravka, bombardier; Sgt. Harold Ripslinger, engineer / top turret gunner; Sgt. Robert LaMotte, radio operator; Sgt. Guy Shelly, left waist gunner; Sgt. Vernon Moore, right waist gunner; and Sgt. Sam Adams, tail turret gunner. They stand by the tail of Zip, the B-24D they flew across the Atlantic from Topeka, Kansas, in February 1943. Zip was painted in factory "dunes tan" in San Diego, California, unlike in Lady Be Good's repaint from olive drab to desert pink in Texas.

1Lt. Bill Hatton stands next to the left waist gun position of his B-24D Zip (serial number 42-40081) at Topeka, Kansas, in February 1943.

Hatton leans out of the pilot's window of Zip at Topeka, Kansas, in February 1943.

The crew of Zip posing for the camera next to the left main landing gear at Topeka, Kansas, in February 1943. Note the long-range 75-gallon fuel tanks in the forward bomb bay installed for the trip across the Atlantic.

Lt. Hatton's crew posing by the tail of their plane Zip.

1Lt. Bill Hatton

Lt. Bob Toner

Left to right: Vernon Moor, Dp Hayes, John Woravka, Guy Shelly, and Harold Ripslinger clowning around next to Zip's bomb bay doors, Topeka, Kansas, February 1943.

CHAPTER 3 LT. HATTON'S CREW

CHAPTER 4 ★ THE MISSION

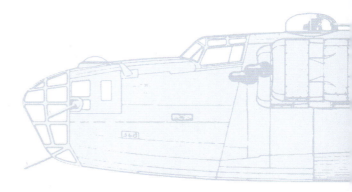

Mission no. 109 for the 376th Bomb Group was slated for an attack on Naples Harbor on the west coast of Italy, on April 4, 1943. The group was to put up twenty-five B-24s from its four squadrons at Soluch, and the aircraft were to be flown in two sections, "A" and "B." They were to hit the target at high altitude at dusk, then break formation and return to Soluch individually at lower altitude under the cover of darkness. For this mission they would not be escorted by fighters (there were no long-range P-51s and P-47s in the Mediterranean theater until months later) and had to depend on their own armament and tactics to outfight day fighter–interceptors on the way to the target, and night fighters on their return to Soluch.

The target was some 750 miles northwest of their base, and the course took them through the Straits of Messina, between Sicily and the heel of the Italian boot; a 1,500-mile round trip. If the 376th aircraft couldn't hit the target before dark, they were to bomb Crotone, on the instep of the Italian boot on the southwest edge of the Gulf of Taranto. The mission should take around nine hours and thirty minutes flying, and with the extra fuel from the bomb bay tank, they should have twenty-one hours of flying time. But because the total mission was less than half the plane's maximum range, they probably didn't have their tanks topped off. But because of strong headwinds on the return leg, two of the crews reported forced landings at Malta, two-thirds of the way back to Soluch, because of fuel shortage.

After lifting off from the dust-choked runway at Soluch, Hatton and Toner turned the Lady Be Good with throttles wide open and climbed up to their assigned altitude. There they formed up with the Liberators of Lieutenants Gluck (#95), Feeley (#72), and Swarners (#90) in the second element of B section, 514th Bomb Squadron.

APRIL 4, 1943

SECTION A

Section A got off the ground at Soluch in a sandstorm at 1330 Benghazi time. The section began with twelve aircraft, but only eleven ships made the full trip. The twelfth returned because of engine and supercharger troubles, aggravated by the sandstorm.

Section B became airborne between 1345 and 1350. From the records, it has been possible to determine that one element of four planes, and three elements of three planes each, originally made up the section.

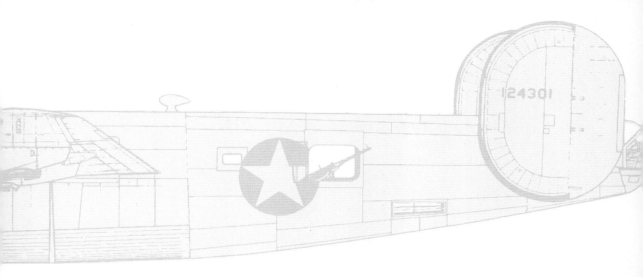

Of twenty-five planes that originally took off to form the two sections, four had to return fairly soon with one or two engines out because of blowing sand. (Soluch was merely an open, flat sandy spot on the edge of the desert. Two days later, the 376th Group moved to a paved airfield at nearby Berka 2.)

Section A was led by Maj. R. A. Soukup. His eleven aircraft hit Naples at 1940 as planned, from 23,000 feet. Antiaircraft fire was heavy, intense, and accurate and hit every one of the eleven B-24s. None were shot down, although several men were wounded. Twelve German fighters climbed to intercept them and had three of their own number shot down by their own antiaircraft guns. The fighters gave up, but the bombers hit Naples Harbor with extreme accuracy, as was shown later in aerial photos.

The B-24 of Lt. Paul J. Fallon (Section A) was hit twenty-one times over the target and had two control cables shot away. Interviewed on July 8, 1959, he stated that this element broke formation into single ships after hitting the target and returned to Soluch at low altitude to avoid Junkers Ju 88 night fighters. It was Fallon's third mission (he flew forty-nine, until shot down over Athens, Greece, eventually escaping through the underground and returning home). He remembered distinctly that Section B pilots said they never got to the target that night. All eleven B-24s of Section A either got back to Soluch or landed on the British island of Malta.

SECTION B

The lead plane of Section B was flown by Capt. M. R. Walsh. The section was divided into two elements of two flights each. In the first element there were four aircraft in the first flight (Walsh's), and three in the second flight (Maj. J. E. Lavin's). The second element was composed of two flights of three ships each: Lt. E. J. Feely led the first flight, and Lt. F. W. Milam led the second. In all, the section included thirteen aircraft.

The section took off from Soluch at 0145. Lt. Hatton, in plane #64, flew number 2 position (right wing) in Lt. Feely's first flight, second element.

As Section B headed north toward Sicily, engine troubles resulting from the sandstorm at takeoff began to plague the planes. At 1700, three aircraft fell out of the formation and went back to Soluch: Lt. Britt's aircraft (#2, second flight, first element) sprung gas leaks in #2 engine and the bomb bay gas tanks; Lt. F. C. Wright (#3, first flight, second element) lost #4 engine first, then #2 went out, and then he got #4 restarted at low altitude and went home on three engines; ten minutes later, Maj. Lavin's plane sprung an oil leak in #1 engine, and the propeller was feathered before returning to Soluch.

At 1840, Lt. Milam, leading the last flight, had his #4 propeller run away and had to feather that propeller and return. Five minutes later, Lt. K. P. Iverson, flying #4 position in the first flight, first element, lost both #1 and #4 engines and left the formation.

Then at 1900, as the section passed the volcanic island of Stromboli, the leaders of both the first and second elements dropped out. Capt. Walsh couldn't get enough performance from his engines to complete the Naples run, so he peeled off to lower altitude and tried to hit Crotone—the secondary target. Weather obscured the target, so he dropped his bombs on a freighter off the cost of Italy and returned to Soluch. The second element leader, Lt. Feely, lost #3 supercharger and feathered the engine—salvoing his bombs in the water to try to keep up with the formation. Then Feely's #3 engine went out and he returned to Soluch.

At 1900, only six of the original thirteen planes of Section B were still headed for the target. There were two flights of three planes each; the first flight was led by Lt. W. M. McCain at this point, and Lt. Hatton apparently was leading the second flight.

At 1920, Lt. D. E. Lear, flying on Hatton's right wing, reported that his waist gunner's oxygen mask froze, so he dived down to 14,000 feet to revive the man, who had become unconscious. Lear lost the formation and flew over Crotone to drop his bombs. Over the target he ran into severe weather, searchlights, and antiaircraft fire. His plane was hit, and his gyro instruments went out. At this point he returned home to Soluch with his bombs.

At 1925, the acting lead ship, piloted by Lt. McCain, found that one of his waist gunner's and his tail gunner's oxygen masks had frozen. One was unconscious and the other in bad shape. So he dived to 15,000 feet to revive the men, lost the formation, and returned home.

Lt. Hatton had assumed lead of the remaining four airplanes at 1925, according to the mission report by Lt. L. A. Worley, who was flying number 2 position (right wing) by this time. The two other aircraft still in formation were flown by Lt. Swarner and Lt. Gluck. The three pilots are unanimous that the lead plane (#64) took them to a point about 30 miles south of Naples, over Sorrento, Italy, at about 1950—approximately fifteen minutes after the sun had set at 25,000 feet. It was then so dark that Hatton apparently decided the four pilots could not see well enough to bomb the target. At least, Lt. Worley and Lt. Gluck both reported they thought that the target would be impossible to hit in the dark. So the lead ship turned south for Soluch and the formation broke up. Possibly, the leader's engines—like those of nine other aircraft in Section B—had begun to act up because of sand inhaled on takeoff.

It was dark, there was absolute radio silence, and the other pilots had no way of knowing for sure why the lead ship turned back.

Lt. Gluck landed at Malta at 2245, low on fuel. Lt. Swarner made it back to Soluch at 2245, and Lt. Worley landed at Soluch at 2310.

An hour and two minutes after Worley landed, the Benina, Libya, HF/DF (high frequency / direction finder) radio station (just east of Benghazi) reported a bearing of 330 degrees (north-northwest) on Hatton's B-24. From the records, and from the memories of living members of the squadron, it is not possible to learn if Benina identified Hatton because of an emergency voice transmission, or if he had turned his IFF (identification, friend or foe) radio to emergency transmission, or if the station simply knew the plane's normal IFF transmission was plane #64 because it was the only aircraft unaccounted for. At any rate, this is the last record of the aircraft's position.

On a bearing of 330 degrees from Benina radio, Hatton was exactly on course for Soluch. He was also forty-two minutes later than all the rest of the aircraft, which landed at Soluch. Why? No one knows for sure.

Apparently, Hatton continued on his southeast course for another two and a half to three hours until his B-24 ran out of fuel, because the scene of the crash site is almost directly on a northwest–southeast line from Soluch. If this is true, the B-24 flew almost directly over Soluch.

Since the plane's radio ADF compass (automatic direction finder) was in operating order when the plane was found, it should have shown the pilot when he was passing Benina. Several pilots returning that night reported the beacon "strong and accurate," and two pilots reported "weak and accurate" reception.

Since the weather was hazy, it is possible, discounting the radio compass, to believe that Hatton could have flown over the coastline and missed identifying it. The desert and the sea look almost identical on a hazy dark night, so, judging from the B-24's continuing on its southeast heading until it ran out of fuel, it is possible to assume that Hatton still thought the plane to be over the Mediterranean—probably attributing what he thought to be slow ground speed to an extremely strong headwind.

Hatton and his crew flew on in the darkness, undoubtedly wondering why they hadn't seen their base yet. Their assumption that they had a stiff headwind would account for the long duration of their flight, so they stayed on the same heading, not knowing they'd already passed over their base in the dark and were heading deeper and deeper into the desert.

When Hatton and his crew never returned to base that night, the next morning an air-sea rescue search went out at 0800, April 5, 1943, on a heading of 330 degrees from Benina out over the Mediterranean. The results of the search on this course were negative. There were several ground personnel at the base who heard a B-24 fly over the base well after the last plane landed at 2330; Capt. Harry Hines, the 514th's engineering officer, was one of these men and early the next morning told Lt. Bill McCain and his copilot Ken Snow, who were also in Section B on the raid, that he thought what they heard fly over the base at almost midnight was Hatton's plane. With this information, McCain and Snow, along with their crew, took it upon themselves, without telling the 514th's squadron commander Capt. Hal Simmons, to do a search mission of their own, but in the opposite direction from the air-sea rescue personnel. So, on a heading of 150 degrees from their base, the reciprocal of the 330-degree bearing provided by the Benina DF Station, McCain and his crew took off that morning flying southeast for over 200 miles into the desert, finding nothing, not ever realizing that they *were* on the right track and the right course, just nowhere near far enough to save their friends. At the 200-mile point, McCain turned his B-24 back toward their base, ending their search.

In late 1944, a board of investigation recommended that Lt. Hatton and his crew be considered "missing in action and presumed dead."

On April 10, 1946, after going through all German and Italian military records and making a search of the Italian coastline (including the interviewing of fishermen along the coast), it was deemed that Lt. Hatton's crew had been "killed in action."

Then, on June 15, 1948, a seven-officer board of inquiry representing the American Graves Registration Service met in Rome, Italy, and declared, after having reviewed the entire case and examining all records accumulated since the war, that all possible efforts had been made to find Lt. Hatton's crew. The crew was presumed to have crashed into the Mediterranean Sea without leaving a trace. As far as the United States military was concerned, the book was closed on the disappearance of B-24D 41-24301, Lt. Hatton, and his crew.

376th Bomb Group, 514th Bomb Squadron's quarters at Berka 2, Libya.

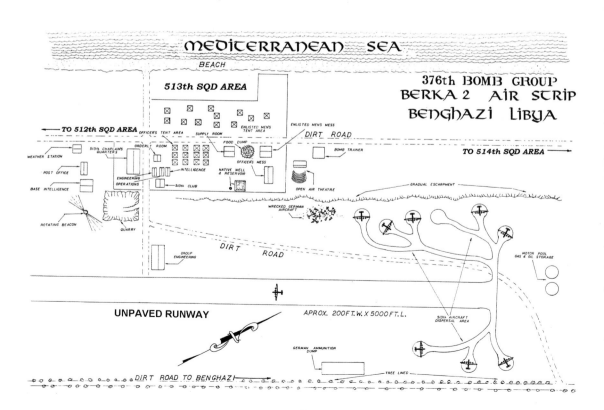

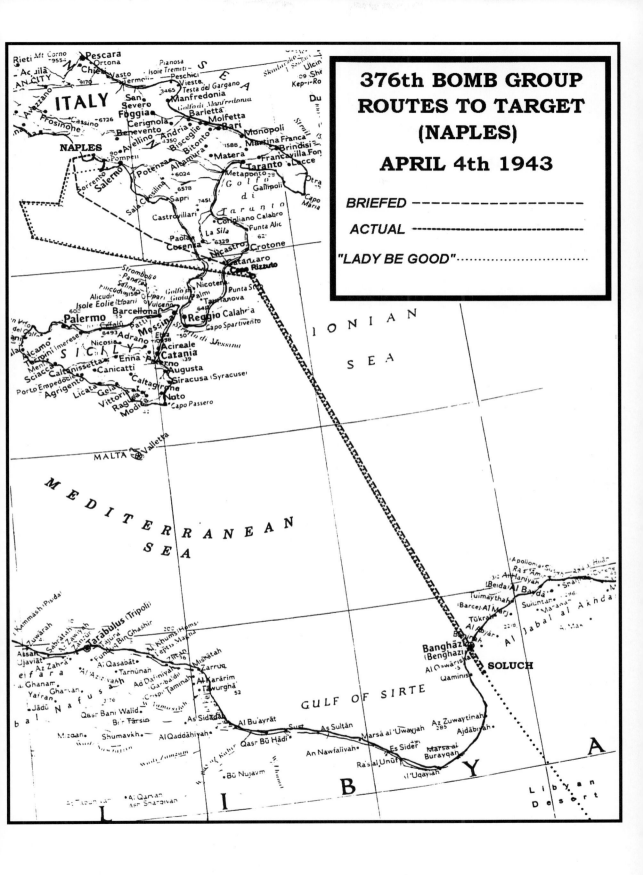

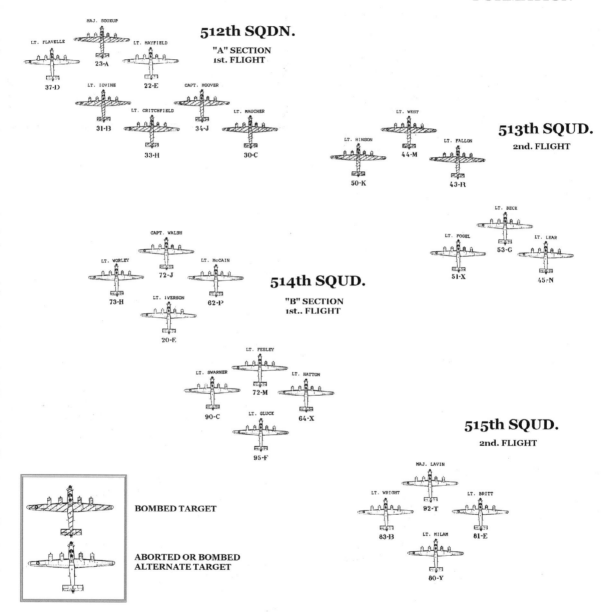

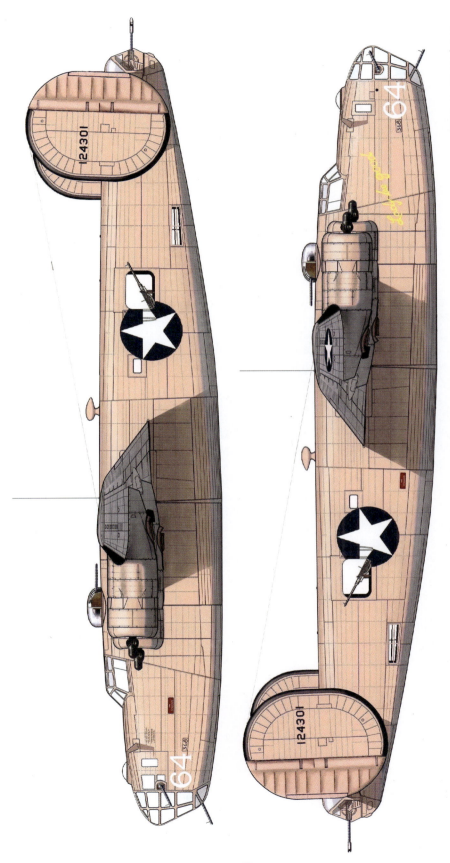

CHAPTER 5 ★ BAILOUT

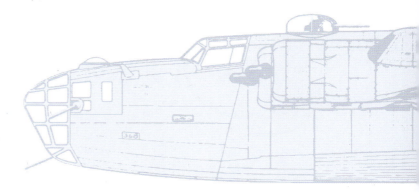

No one knows what really happened aboard the B-24 at the end of their long flight out across the Libyan Desert, but after examination of the aircraft, the disposition of the items aboard, and what would have been called on by the crew for a bailout, learned during their training, the following is supposition as to what *may* have transpired in those last moments.

As the engines ran out of fuel one at a time, Lt. Hatton would have shut off all switches and fuel to these engines and feathered the props. With the #4 engine still having enough fuel to pull them through the night sky, Lt. Hatton came to the conclusion that their time was up; they would have to bail out before they wouldn't have enough altitude to do so. Hatton must have shared these thoughts with his copilot, Bob Toner, then made a joint decision. Calling out to the crew on the aircraft intercom, bailout procedure was gone over and verified with each crew member, then the order was given. First out would probably have been the bombardier, John Woravka, and the navigator, Dp Hays, both in the nose. Hatton would have opened the bomb bay doors, then Harold Ripslinger, the aircraft engineer and top turret gunner, would have made his way off the flight deck, where the pilot and copilot were, and climbed down to the bomb bay, where he could have made a quick exit out the bottom of the plane.

Lt. Toner probably had made his way down to the bomb bay compartment with Sgt. Ripslinger, then across the catwalk back through the bomb bay to the waist gun positions to check on the status of the four other men in the tail. Hatton, as plane commander, was still at the Lady's controls to make last-minute adjustments to the trim tabs in order to compensate for the torque of the one outboard engine still operating, on the right wing. The autopilots installed in B-24Ds at that time were notoriously unreliable, so after setting the mixture controls on the #4 engine, Hatton was satisfied he had done all he could do, and at that, he took his throat mike off and discarded it down between his seat and the bulkhead to his left. He removed his headset and laid it across the pilot's yoke column, stood up, removed his Colt .45 gun belt, and carefully laid it on his seat; thinking now, as aircraft commander, that he had satisfied his duty of being the last man off his plane, he turned and made his way down to the open bomb bay.

Toner and the rest of the crew had already bailed out of the belly entrance hatch, and as Hatton stood on the catwalk, where the plane's bombload once had hung just a few short hours before, the only sounds were the empty bomb shackles' metallic clinking against the bomb racks, the whistling of the wind below him, and the lone Pratt & Whitney engine still running smoothly. Bill Hatton may have turned for the

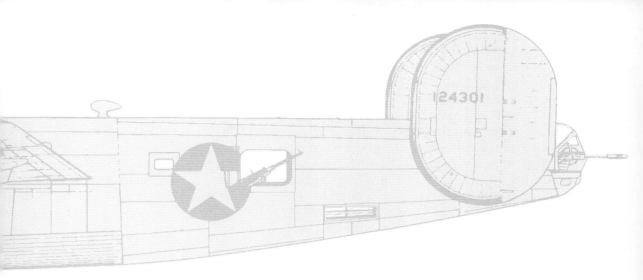

last time to look back up into the cockpit, where he saw the dim green glow of the instruments and may have wondered, "What will happen to us now?" Turning back, he took a breath, side-stepped the catwalk, and dropped into the inky blackness.

It must have been a big surprise to each crew member as they floated down in the cold, 0200 pitch blackness, any second expecting to hit cold seawater, but instead, with a bone-jarring thud, impacting solid ground.

Within a few minutes of landing, the crew members would have started to call out to each other in the dark, one or two, and firing a flare, which helped link all of them up into a group as per their training, all except John Woravka, the bombardier.

Exhausted, they would have bedded down for the night and, for a cushion and warmth, slept in their high-altitude flight suits.

The next morning after waking, the crew would have first taken stock of any water or food they had with them, as per their training, which was two canteens each, probably half full, and a few odd pieces of candy, then would have started looking for the bombardier, Lt. John Woravka. We now know they never found him.

The Lady Be Good, with no one at her controls, sustained level flight, but with only the #4 engine running, and Hatton's trim settings, she couldn't sustain her altitude. Slowly, she dropped lower and lower, turning in a wide arc counterclockwise, flying on for another 16 miles, until there was no more altitude. In the darkness, no one saw her impact the desert plateau, but on the basis of what the first US Air Force investigation team saw at the crash site during their inspection in May 1959, and all the photos taken at that time, this is the sequence of events.

First contact with the ground was made by the #4 propeller, spinning at around 2,000 rpm cruise setting. It tore into the sand, wrenching it from the prop shaft and sending it cart-wheeling off into the darkness; the torque also tore off the entire #4 engine just behind the exhaust manifolds, sending it bouncing along in the same direction and spewing cowling parts. Next contact was the lower-nose "chin" .50-caliber machine gun barrel, which promptly bent it at a 90-degree angle, jamming it back up next to the left cheek gun. She settled onto her belly with a thud, tearing off her rolled-up bomb bay doors and bomb racks.

With her belly collapsed, her remaining three props made contact. The #1, #2, and #3 engines were shut down, with the propellers in the feathered position, so, other than bent prop blades and the #1 engine being bent slightly up at the engine mounts, they had little damage.

The plane was turning clockwise at the moment of impact, causing it to continue its rotation or "spin" in that direction, like a top. The bottom of the right wingtip tore through some debris flung off the #4 engine, tearing a gash in the skin in an arch from the bottom of the right wingtip to the US national insignia.

While spinning, the vertical stabilizers rocked back and forth, damaging the bottom of the right one and finally digging into the sand on the left stabilizer, folding it in half just below the left horizontal stabilizer and causing the aircraft to come to an abrupt wrenching halt, but not before the stresses of turning and twisting caused the fuselage to split and tear in half at a bulkhead just behind the trailing edge of the wings; this was considered a weak point in B-24s. From the time of impact to the end of her slide, she covered close to 1,000 feet.

After she stopped her grinding slide across the desert floor, the silence would have been deafening; all you would have heard would have been the whisper of a light breeze blowing a few inches off the pebble-strewn surface.

Dawn came some three hours later, with the first rays of light reflecting off the Lady's nose and windscreen.

As she was flying south-southeast and turning in an arc, she had come all the way around in a westerly direction and bellied in on the plateau. Because she was rotating on impact after making contact with the ground, she came to a stop facing east-southeast, in the direction she had made first contact with the ground, pointing her nose toward all the debris and parts that were flung off. The #4 propeller had come to a stop shortly after separating from the shaft and was the farthest away from Lady Be Good, with her hub pointing up.

When the #4 engine was ripped from its mounts, it bounced along the surface, "chasing" Lady Be Good, and ended up stopping its roll just short of hitting the B-24 between its #1 and #2 engines. It landed inverted, with the back row of cylinders and the exhaust collector ring pointing up out of the sand. The nosewheel ended up being torn out of its compartment, ending up halfway between Lady Be Good and its #4 propeller. There were pieces of the bomb racks and the rolled-up bomb bay doors scattered the length of the debris field, along with the reduction-gearing assembly and the magnetos that had been attached to the back of the #4 engine, and large pieces of the engine cowling.

The Lady Be Good crashed on a sand and gravel plateau approximately 440 miles south-southeast of the Libyan coast at Benghazi. This location is only 500 feet above sea level. About 70 miles to the north, and in a "U" shape around the plane on three sides, is the impassible Libyan Sand Sea. To the south, 100 miles away, is a 2,300-foot mountain range that seals off the south of the "U" formed by the sand sea. It is apparently impossible to escape the plateau either by foot or on camelback. Wheelus Air Base officials in 1959 reported that even the desert nomads never visit the area (and certainly no one came upon the B-24 in the sixteen years she lay there, because its supplies were absolutely intact).

Beyond the sand sea, there are several bases at distances that would have been impossible for the men to reach. To the northwest, 150 miles from where the men landed, is the Gialo Oasis. South-southeast 155 miles is El Giof Oasis, and 170 miles north-northeast is the Oasis of Siwa, in Egypt. Air Force experts at Wheelus Air Base estimate that sun temperatures in the area in April average 135 degrees plus. There is no vegetation or shade of any sort. Capt. James M. Paule, an Air Force flight surgeon who investigated at the scene, estimated that a man could last only two days with all the water he could carry. And since there is positive evidence that the crew never found their aircraft, all they had was whatever water was left in the canteens that some of the crew bailed out with. Probably the 50 miles of marked trails they left would be a near-absolute limit of endurance.

The B-24 bellied in 258 miles south-southeast of the wreckage of an RAF Lancaster and an American B-25 bomber found by the British in 1958, 45 miles north of Giarabub Oasis, Egypt. American crewmen from the B-25 were found by US Army searchers led by Wesley A. Neep, who was a member of the B-24 search team. British crewmen from the Lancaster bomber were found buried beside their bomber—probably by nomads.

After checking on the men in the tail, Lt. Toner adjusts his parachute harness in preparation for bailout. Exiting through the aft belly hatch first would be tail gunner Sgt. Adams, followed by Sgt. Moore and Shelly, then Sgt. LaMotte. Lt. Toner, being the only officer in the tail, would have bailed out last.

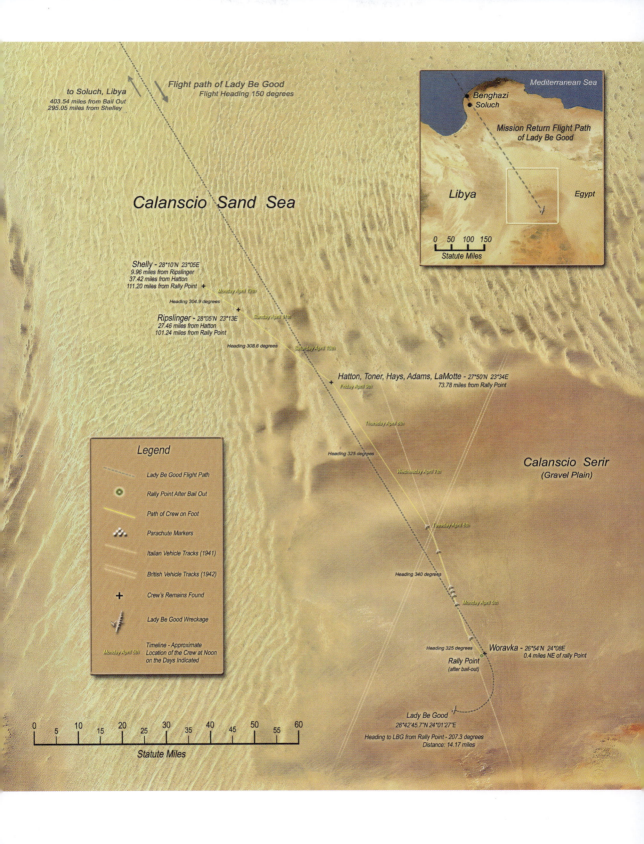

CHAPTER 5 BAILOUT

CHAPTER 6 ★ THE DISCOVERY

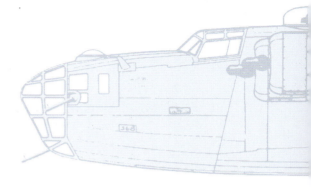

By shear fate, on April 17, 1958, while flying out over an uncharted area of the Libyan Desert in a Douglas C-47 jointly owned and operated by the D'Arcy Exploration Company and the British Petroleum Company (now known as BP), Charles Hellewell and his fellow British oil explorers, by chance, sighted something far below them on the desert floor. The geologists aboard the plane were out looking for surface features that might be an indication of oil-bearing strata for future oil drilling. What they saw below was an airplane, resting on a featureless gravel plain. This location wasn't anywhere near any aircraft flight routes over North Africa.

Hellewell took a rough fix of the aircraft's location some 385 miles from Tobruk, Libya, to later be passed along to the D'Arcy ground survey parties because they were slated to be in the area looking for oil within the next year or so. Some seven months later, on November 9, 1958, the aircraft was spotted again by Ronald McLean on another survey flight by D'Arcy. This time they had the pilot fly lower and circled to get a better look at what they saw, which turned out to be a World War II four-engine bomber with the US Army Air Force white star in a blue circle on its wing and fuselage.

From the air, it looked like the crew had done a pretty good job of setting the plane down for a belly landing. McLean took an astrofix of the aircraft's location and entered the geographical coordinates into his logbook; they then continued on to their base at the El Giof airstrip in Kufra, where the next D'Arcy ground survey team had come down from Benghazi on the coast and was slated to leave for their next oil exploratory trip out into the desert. McLean turned the location information over to the three surveyors, John Martin, Don Sheridan, and Gordon Bowerman, who were going to explore the area south of the aircraft sighting.

On the face of it, there wasn't any hurry to find this plane, only because there were many aircraft wrecks scattered across North Africa that were left over from the war, which had ended on that continent more than sixteen years earlier, so this aircraft was just one of many, and the fact that D'Arcy wasn't paying these men to go out of their way to investigate wrecked aircraft left over from the war. So by the middle of February 1959, and with over a month's load of supplies in their Dodge Power Wagon, Land Rover, and a 3-ton Bedford truck, Martin, Sheridan, and Bowerman with their three Libyan truck drivers, Sayid bin Ramadan, Ali Shariff, and Abdul Gealil (it was illegal for Europeans to drive in Libya), headed north from the Kufra Oasis, surveying for oil.

One of these derelict aircraft left over from World War II was a British RAF Bristol Blenheim Mk. IV twin-engine bomber, which had been discovered by Sheridan and Martin two months before. The exploration team came across this aircraft again

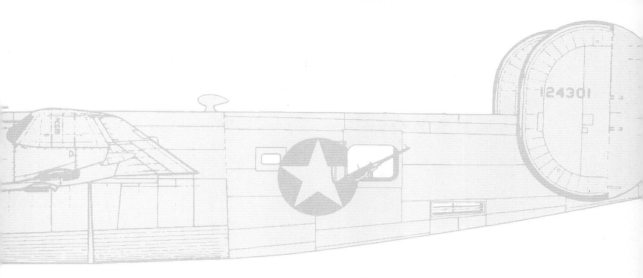

on February 23, 60 miles northeast of Kufra. The bomber's crew had made a successful wheels-down landing on the desert floor back on May 5, 1942, after getting lost and separated from two other Blenheims while conducting a navigation training mission out over the desert.

After running out of fuel while trying to make it to Kufra, the crew stayed with the plane after landing, hoping for rescue, which came four days too late on May 9, 1942. A Vickers Wellington found the Blenheim (Z7513), landed, and discovered the three-man crew all stretched out in the shade of one of the wings, dead; they had died of dehydration.

The bodies of the three crewmen were buried, marked by three 55-gallon oil drums. The aircraft was left where it landed, and rediscovered in 1959. The bodies of the three crewmen were exhumed in 1959 by the British Long Range Desert Group and reburied in Knightsbridge War Cemetery at Acroma, Libya.

By the end of the month, the oil exploration team had entered a limitless, flat, sand-and-gravel plateau that stretched out as far as they could see. This plateau was surrounded on three sides by massive sand dunes called the Calanscio Serir Dunes. There was no vegetation whatsoever on what lay before them; other than the blue sky, it could have been the surface of Mars. The three Brits had never seen anything like this in all their travels; the temperature was rising above 130 degrees by noon and making it difficult to even breath the superheated air. But because of the hard-packed and level ground, they started to make good time traveling north toward the general vicinity of the coordinates given them by McLean. Referring to these coordinates, the three vehicles turned northeast. Arriving at that location on the late afternoon of February 27, they found nothing, so they spread the three vehicles out as far as they could go while keeping each in sight, in a line going northeast. By 1730 (almost sunset), Bowerman, after five days of exploring the desert for oil deposits, saw the distinctive twin tails of the B-24 in the distance. The three vehicles pulled up a short time later and stopped a few yards away, cutting their engines. All you could hear was the light breeze at ground level.

The sun had just set, with the ambient light left over fading to darkness fast, so the six men bedded down for the night, exhausted and hungry from traveling almost 170 miles since sunup. The anticipation of the next day's treasure hunt for the Libyans as well as the Brits was rampant, but after the evening meal and setting up their cots for the night, they were all fast asleep in a short time.

The next morning they were all up at sunrise and ready to see what treasures they might be able to "liberate" from the American bomber. As they approached toward the nose, they could make out the stylized letters "Good" at an angle below the cockpit on the right side, and on closer inspection in the crushed section of the fuselage below the word "Good," they could make out the letters "ady Be," surmising the entire name being the song "Lady Be Good." There was also the number "64" painted in white on the lower forward section of the nose.

Walking around to the left side of the nose, they could see nothing written there except the number "64" on the extreme lower forward section, like on the right side. Sheridan looked at the entire crash site and thought the plane had come down in level flight and hit the desert floor in a slight rotation clockwise, skidding along till the left stabilizer dug into the sand, abruptly stopping the skid and rotation and breaking the fuselage in half just behind the trailing edge of the wings. By opening the dorsal hatch just behind the top of the cockpit, two of the six men scrambled into the plane, finding several items of interest and value: two Colt .45-caliber handguns still in their US holsters and web belts (one of these was sitting on the pilot's seat, exactly where Lt. Hatton had laid it sixteen years before), two .30-caliber bolt action Springfield rifles, and a .45-caliber Thomson submachine gun. What they didn't find was any trace of the crew; it looked to them like the crew had bailed out, considering the empty individual parachute bags that were lying around inside the wreckage. After climbing up on the left wing and walking to the fuselage, Sheridan and Martin noticed two compartment hatches between the wings; thinking there was something inside, they had one of the Libyans get a pry bar off one of the trucks to pry these compartments open, not noticing the recessed spring-loaded handles just behind the hatches, which when popped up could be turned 90 degrees to open the hatches. Instead, they pried and pried at the hatch groves until they gouged large-enough dents, shoving the pry bars farther in, and broke the hatches open.

With these two compartments open, what Sheridan, Martin, and the Libyans found made them smile with satisfaction; each compartment contained a hand-cranked "Gibson Girl" emergency transmitter radio, complete with a box kite antenna for each one, four sealed pint containers of water in each compartment, weather balloons, and life rafts, the latter complete with oars and small covers to seal against rainstorms at sea. All these items were taken and loaded into their vehicles by the Libyans. After finding the small US arsenal inside the aircraft's forward section, Ali and Sayid huddled together, talking excitedly in Arabic and, with big grins on their faces, handling the American weapons, undoubtedly thinking these were now their property. As they progressed through the fuselage and tail section, they found the mummified carcasses of several wayward birds that had gotten lost flying across the desert and used the shade to rest, only to die where they had landed.

Taking stock of the .50-caliber machine guns and ammo, it looked like all of it was there and intact. With all the parachutes gone, it was evident the crew had bailed out and the bomber came down by itself. Bowerman made notes of the names he found on items in the fuselage—Lt. Hatton, Lt. Woravka, Lt. Hays, Lt. Toner, Sgt. Ripslinger, and a Sgt. Shea's name written on an envelope found on the floor near one of the waist guns; it was later determined that Sgt. Shea wasn't part of the crew. They also found the maintenance inspection log with the aircraft call sign ("64"), squadron number (514th). and bomb group number (376th). Some of the other items that were removed by Martin and Bowerman along with all the weapons were the master compass, globe compass in the cockpit, signal flare pistols, sextant, chronometer, the navigator's case of books, maps, flight bags, escape maps, parallel rulers, dividers, wind drift calculator, and anything else that looked like it had some value.

By 1000 on February 28, the heat was so intense they all felt it was time to break camp, load everything up along with what they had taken from the plane, and head out for their next location, Mushroom Rocks to the south. One last thing Bowerman did just before he climbed into the Land Rover was walk over to the tail and jot down the serial number written on the vertical stabilizer, 124301. After finishing their surveys in the desert, which involved having a good time when camped at night by firing off the flair pistols they had taken from the bomber, by March 12 the team headed back to Kufra. After their arrival, the Brits made immediate plans to head back to the coast at Benghazi. Prior to leaving on their 600-mile trip back to the coast, Sheridan took all the weapons they had liberated from the Lady Be Good down to the local police station and used them to bribe the police chief, Senussi, as a trade for extra gasoline and special commercial driver's licenses so the three Englishmen could drive themselves without Libyan drivers. The police chief was happy to make that trade and took all the American weapons. This really upset Ali and Sayid, who thought that the guns and ammo were theirs.

By March 15, the three Englishmen set out for the coast, which they reached by March 21, then flew to Tripoli to give the D'Arcy Corporation their report on the oil findings, never letting on about the detour they took to locate the American bomber and all the items they took from the plane. The extra gasoline they used for this detour was replaced with the fuel they got from the police chief in Kufra on the "trade" for the American weapons from the Lady Be Good.

What they took from the American bomber was stored in boxes in a spare room of an apartment supplied by D'Arcy for its employees in Tripoli. Very few people knew about their discovery of the plane and its contents, and the last thing they wanted was to have to explain their detour and the extra three days in the desert, as well as what they had taken from the plane. Both Sheridan and Martin felt it really wasn't necessary to inform the Americans at Wheelus Air Force Base about the discovery of one of their bombers from World War II.

Apparently, after talking to his wife, who attended the same Christian church as a US Air Force lieutenant colonel, Walter Kolbus, from the air force base at Wheelus, Gordon Bowerman, just prior to leaving for his next assignment with D'Arcy, sent a letter to Col. Kolbus outlining the American bomber they had found in the desert back in February. He gave him the names they had found on the parachute bags, as well as the serial number on the tail; this was on April 2, 1959. Bowerman was still concerned as to whether the crew had ever been rescued, and asked Col. Kolbus if he could check US Air Force records.

Col. Kolbus turned all this information in the letter over to the Wheelus operations personnel, who gave the latitude and longitude that Bowerman included in the letter to Wheelus's search and rescue. They plotted the location and found that there was no relief data available on any of the maps that deep into the Libyan Desert; it had never been explored until the D'Arcy oil team had traversed it.

Wheelus officials contacted their headquarters in Wiesbaden, Germany, letting them know of the discovery and asking if they had any records on the plane. Since no records were kept in Europe, Wiesbaden contacted the Pentagon in Washington, DC, the Army Military Records Center in St. Louis, and Maxwell Air Force Base Historical Research Center. Information on B-24D, serial number 41-24301, came back as missing in action on April 4, 1943; no trace of the plane or crew was ever found. After this information was relayed back to Air Force headquarters in Wiesbaden, they contacted the Army's Office of the Quartermaster General on April 24, which contacted their Mortuary System in Frankfurt, Germany. This unit was responsible for the recovery and identification of World War II casualties wherever they were found. They were immediately ordered to proceed to the crash site of the missing bomber, with the goal of finding and recovering the remains of the crew.

On May 4, Col. Kolbus sent a letter to Bowerman, letting him know that an investigation team from the US Army's Office of the Quartermaster General Mortuary System was on its way to Tripoli to talk to him and should be arriving there by May 13. However, Bowerman was out on another assignment for D'Arcy, so he didn't receive the letter until after the team arrived in Tripoli.

Capt. Myron (Chuck) Fuller, of the US Army's Office of the Quartermaster General Mortuary System, and Wesley A. Neep, a contracted civilian who was, after twenty-five years, hands down the best forensic-identification specialist in his field, headed the QMS team that had arrived in Tripoli from Frankfurt, Germany. They proceeded to the D'Arcy offices in Tripoli to interview Gordon Bowerman, but he hadn't returned from the field yet, so the D'Arcy people had them meet with Sheridan and Martin, who gave Fuller and Neep an outline of how the bomber was spotted from the air the previous year, and then, after getting the position from the pilot, how the three oilmen were able, with some difficulty, to locate the plane after traversing that uncharted part of the desert. Both Sheridan and Martin stressed that going to Blockhouse Rock first was a must to get the correct bearings to the American bomber. Blockhouse Rock was the only landmark in the area, a solitary limestone outcropping rising some 25 feet from the desert floor, situated near the west side of the plateau midway up at the edge of the Sand Sea of Calanscio Serir Dunes, which surrounded the plateau on the west, north, and part of the east sides. They also gave the Americans an overlay map of the area and the coordinates of the bomber's location. One thing Sheridan and Martin didn't tell Fuller and Neep about was the items they took from the plane.

After this meeting, Capt. Fuller contacted the commander of the 7272nd Air Base Wing at Wheelus Air Force Base, requesting light planes and helicopters be provided to the QMS investigators for the examination of the B-24 and the search for the crew. After arriving at Wheelus, the team found that the base commander had no interest in providing them with any help in getting down to the crash site, 750 miles from his base, and they were directed to contact Maj. Harry Hays, operations officer of the 58th Air Rescue Squadron. Hays was interested in the exact location of the bomber, as well as possibly sighting any markers left by the crew, so Maj. Hays gave the team the use of a USAF SC-54 with large observation bubbles on each side of the fuselage, used for search and rescue. The flight left Wheelus on the morning of May 14, navigating to Blockhouse Rock first and then to the crash site, without any problems. While overflying the B-24 wreck at low level several times, Maj. Hays had to fly on instruments because of the lack of a distinct horizon caused by optical shimmering of the desert floor.

The search team saw no trail markers left by the Lady Be Good's crew near the crash site, nor on a flight path heading back in the direction of the bomber's former base at Soluch. Prior to the flight back to Tripoli, the SC-54 flew back to Blockhouse Rock, dumping sacks of lime along the way between the B-24 and Blockhouse Rock for the forthcoming ground search parties. Maj. Hays decided not to land his big four-engine aircraft without knowing if the sand gravel plain would support its weight, so he opted to fly back to Wheelus near Benghazi.

After returning, the team had a nagging question on what happened to the crew. They saw from the low-level overflight of the bomber and its location that the plane was on a direct northwest-to-southeast course following a track not just from their base on the coast, but also from their return course from their intended target on April 4, 1943. To them, this indicated that the crew stayed with the plane for almost the entire flight, at least up to when they were flying on only one engine and starting to lose altitude. It was thought that the navigator's flight log book and maps were still in the plane (the D'Arcy exploration party never indicated they had also taken them) and might shed some light on when and where the crew bailed out. Maj. Hays indicated that he had lighter SC-47s back at the base that might be used to land at the crash site, but also, to be cautious, the US Army's 329th Engineers Map Survey Detachment at Wheelus had several Cessna L-19s to chose from for one to make stops at the oil exploration camps because of the L-19's short range on the way down, with the SC-47 to follow.

So, plans were made and supplies and aircraft were requisitioned for a two-to-three-day stay out on the desolate plateau. The crew was selected for the SC-47: an accomplished photographer (but just about everyone took a camera of some kind), a writer who could transcribe all the information, Chuck Fuller and Wes Neep as the investigators, two very experienced pilots to fly the SC-47, an experienced USAF navigator, a USAF doctor and specialist in forensics, and a couple of air force enlisted men to help out. It was also decided to have a very experienced officer to fly as a passenger in the Army L-19 to determine the suitability of the ground around the crash site to land the SC-47.

RAF Bristol Blenheim Mk. IV Z7513 was rediscovered in February 1959, still sitting up on its landing gear after seventeen years in the desert.

The British Long Range Desert Group examines the Mk. IV after seventeen years in the desert sun.

The three crewmen were exhumed by the British Long Range Desert Group and brought back and reburied in Knightsbridge War Cemetery, Acroma, Libya.

The left side of the B-24's nose, clearly showing the individual aircraft number, "64."

CHAPTER 6 THE DISCOVERY

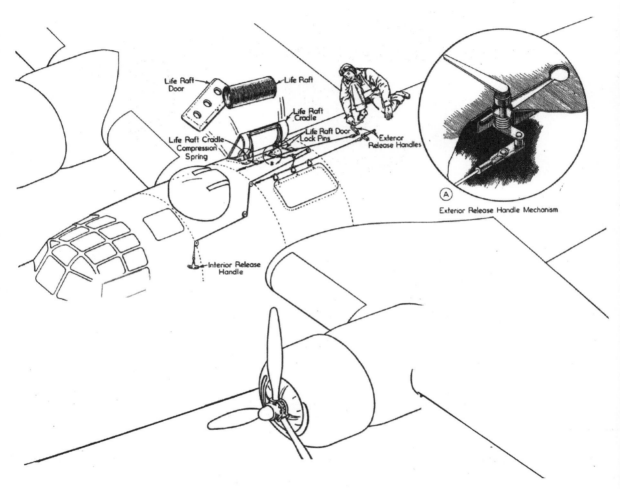

Instructions showing how to open the life raft compartments on a B-24.

This photo shows just how desolate the Sahara Desert looks from the air as the D'Arcy oil exploration aircraft flies lower to get a better look at the Lady Be Good, November 9, 1958.

CHAPTER 6 THE DISCOVERY

Three photos taken on the early morning of February 28, 1959. These are the first photos taken of the Lady Be Good, within minutes of each other, by the BP/D'Arcy oil surveyor Gordon Bowerman.

CHAPTER 6 THE DISCOVERY

Libyan BP oil truck driver Sayid bin Ramadin attempting to pry something off the break in the fuselage. Shortly after this photo was taken (by Gordon Bowerman), the two drivers used a bar to pry open two compartments on the top of the fuselage, just behind the top turret. There is a recessed handle on the top of the fuselage to open these compartments, but this was not used. The compartment held a rubber life raft, a weather balloon, and the "Gibson Girl" hand-cranked emergency radio.

Blockhouse Rock rising 25 feet above the desert floor near the Calanscio dunes.

As the SC-54 approached the crash site from altitude, this view is of the tiny object to the left center, which shows what the desert plateau and the B-24 look like from altitude, and just how difficult it is to see anything from the air.

US Air Force Douglas SC-54C Skymaster Search & Rescue aircraft used to make the first USAF sighting of the Lady Be Good.

Capt. Myron C. Fuller (*with headset*) sits in the observer's seat next to the bulged Plexiglass viewing bubble aboard the SC-54.

Investigator Neep and Capt. Fuller peer out of the observation bubble of the SC-54 as the pilot banks left to give them a better view of the derelict B-24.

Low pass made by the USAF SC-54C Search & Rescue aircraft for a first-time closer look by the Americans.

USAF SC-54 passes low over the derelict bomber for a better look.

CHAPTER 6 THE DISCOVERY

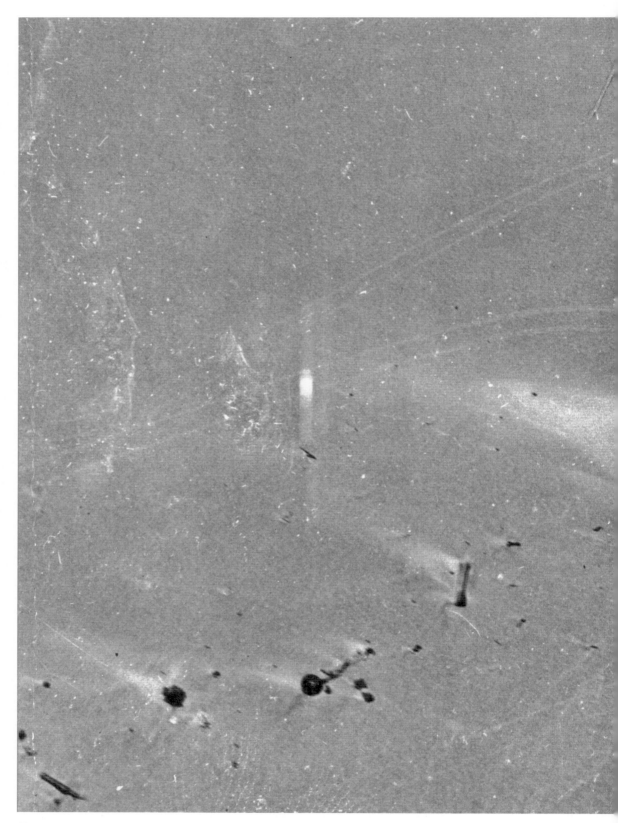
Close aerial view of the debris field left by the B-24 during her corkscrew death slide.

CHAPTER 7 ★ THE FIRST USAF / US ARMY FLIGHT TO THE CRASH SITE

PERSONNEL ABOARD USAF SC-47A, SERIAL NUMBER O-3889	
USAF PILOT	Maj. William F. Rubertus
USAF COPILOT	Capt. Rhea W. Pinkston
USAF NAVIGATOR	Capt. John Post
HEAD OF QUARTERMASTER MORTUARY SYSTEMS FIELD OPERATIONS IN EUROPE US ARMY	Capt. Myron D. Fuller
CIVILIAN IDENTIFICATION SPECIALIST, US ARMY CONTRACTOR	Wesley A. Neep
USAF DOCTOR	Capt. James M. Paule
US ARMY PHOTOGRAPHER	PFC Gilbert Hodne
USAF INFORMATION WRITER	MSgt. Wayne L. Woods
USAF AIRMAN	A1C James M. Meadote
USAF ELECTRONICS SPECIALIST (RADIO)	A1C Russell L. Rafeld

PERSONNEL ABOARD US ARMY CESSNA L-19A, SERIAL NUMBER 14838	
US ARMY PILOT	Lt. Griffen Marr
USAF OBSERVER	Col. H. W. Elder

SUNDAY, MAY 24, 1959

As told through the diary of Wesley Neep, the narrative begins: "Lt. Marr and Col. Elder departed Wheelus Air Force Base and flew to Marble Arch, where they changed aircraft from a Cessna L-19B to an L-19A (serial number 14838), which was ten knots faster. They then flew approx. 150 miles south to Mobil camp #1." The balance of the search team at Wheelus were preparing to depart in Douglas SC-47A (serial number 03889) at 0800, when they received a message from Lt. Griffen Marr saying that he was having trouble with engine overheating and wanted them to bring a change of oil and a new set of spark plugs. He then flew another 75 miles farther south to Mobil camp #2 drilling site, where there was a suitable landing area for the SC-47.

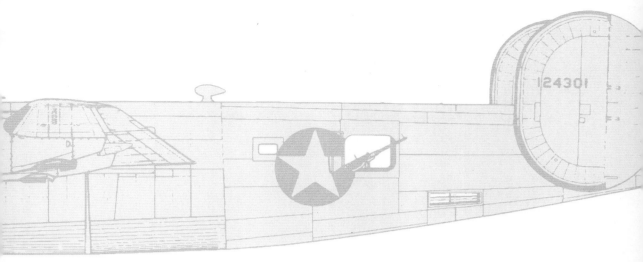

MONDAY, MAY 25, 1959

At 0915, the SC-47 departed Wheelus. At 1200, it arrived over Marble Arch and turned south to follow the course of the L-19. At 1340 they landed at Mobil camp #2. Oil and plugs were changed in the L-19, and a couple of test flights were made. Now the real test came, with the 125-mile flight over the northern area of the Great Sand Sea and then out over the plateau to the Lady Be Good crash site. Lt. Marr and Col. Elder took off and SC-47 followed. The much-faster SC-47 kept circling the slower L-19, shepherding them along the way. Pretty soon, Lt. Marr radioed that he was having engine overheating problems again and was afraid he may have to crash-land in the dunes. Of course, if that happened, we would have a very serious situation. The L-19 would disintegrate on impact with the high, rolling sand dunes. If Lt. Marr and Col. Elder survived a crash, it would be a long delay in getting a helicopter dismantled and flown to Mobil camp #2, then reassembled to fly down to where the L-19 was in the dunes.

The worst fears were over when the L-19 finally made a safe landing at the B-24 crash site. Col. Elder checked out the landing area, gave it his OK, and then the SC-47 landed safely and taxied up near the B-24 and L-19. By the time the engines stopped, it was after 1700, four hours later than the intended landing time. Lt. Marr informed everyone that his L-19 would not be able to fly more than one hour more and would have to be dismantled and brought back to Wheelus in pieces. That pretty much changed the plans to fly test searches by air. Wes discussed with Capt. Fuller that possibly Lt. Marr would be willing to make a test flight early in the morning, when it was still very cool, they put it to Lt. Marr, and he agreed.

At 2100 they began bedding down for the night. Capt. Fuller and Wes watched as the guys placed their bedrolls on the sand-and-pebble surface. Wes indicated that he'd sleep on the left wing.

The wingtip is only 18 inches off the ground, so it was easy to climb up on. Capt. Fuller and Dr. Paule joined Wes on the wingtip, and there was a reason for this. It wasn't very comfortable on the surface of the wing, but it was better than possibly having scorpions or vipers that they heard about crawl into their sleeping bag!

It was a beautiful desert night with a full sky of stars and constellations from horizon to horizon in every direction, something possible only in the open desert or out at sea. By midnight the full moon was overhead and made it almost as bright as daylight. After the moon had traversed the night sky and had dipped below the horizon, Capt. Fuller and Wes got up and went for a one-hour walk to discuss the different star clusters and the arm of the Milky Way galaxy, which were brilliant and plentiful.

The SC-47 lands at Mobil Camp #2 with new oil and spark plugs for the L-19.

Cessna L-19A 14838 parked at Mobil Camp #2, awaiting fresh oil and new spark plugs.

Investigation team deplanes the SC-47 at Mobil Camp #2 to stretch their legs while new oil and spark plugs are installed on the L-19 engine.

Shown here is break in the right side of the fuselage with one of the .50-caliber machine guns visible in the waist gun window.

With the L-19 in the foreground, the search team approaches the Lady Be Good for the first time.

First inspection of the Lady Be Good by the US Air Force and Army search team personnel shortly after landing at the crash site on the late afternoon of May 25, 1959. Col. Elders is standing next to the cockpit, while Maj. Rubertus (*with red hat*) is next to the top turret.

US Army photographer PFC Gilbert Hodne inspects the interior of the tail section shortly after the investigation team landed on the late afternoon of May 25, 1959. Note that there is almost nothing removed or disturbed at the crash site at this time.

Photo taken somewhere around 1730–1800, not long before sunset on May 25.

Photographer PFC Gil Hodne walks around the left wingtip of the Lady Be Good, showing that it was less than 2 feet off the ground and probably the safest place to sleep for the night.

CHAPTER 8 ★ THE INSPECTION

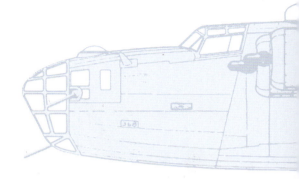

TUESDAY, MAY 26, 1959

By 0600, the search team was up and fixing a breakfast of coffee, eggs, and bacon. Maj. Rubertus had brought his Coleman cook stove, large coffee pot, and 8 mm film camera. In no time, Capt. Fuller and Lt. Marr were up in the L-19 for about fifty minutes while it was still cool. When they landed, Fuller said that it was a no-go searching by air unless you had a grid on the ground for guidance. Fuller said he thought he had spotted something and asked Marr to return for a look-see. They were unable to find what Fuller had spotted. After that flight, the dismantling of the L-19 began. The L-19 wings and tail surfaces were removed and placed in the SC-47. After wheeling the fuselage over to the SC-47's open doors, try as they may to lift and turn the fuselage in, it wouldn't fit. The balance of the aircraft would have to be retrieved on a subsequent trip to the crash site.

While that was going on, Wes Neep made a record of all the parts that had been torn off the B-24 on her 1,000- foot death slide across the desert floor. The landing gear were reattached to the L-19, wheeled over to the B-24's tail assembly, and backed under the right horizontal stabilizer, which afforded it some protection from the blowing desert sand. A 55-gallon drum of fuel was tied to the tail, and a 55-gallon drum of water was tied to the engine to help keep the plane in place. After this project was completed, several of the search team decided to spread out in a wide line, headed northwest, in an initial search effort to look for clues from the missing crew; they were all soon out of sight. A while later, one man could be seen staggering back toward the B-24, and Wes ran out to help him. It was Air Force sergeant Meadote, who when he departed on the search had a cowboy hat on to protect against the brutal sun. The hat had blown off in the wind some time before, which left Meadote unprotected. The heat had affected him to the point where he kept lifting his feet extra high and placing them awkwardly back on the ground, like he was stepping over objects.

Shortly before landing at the crash site, the radio transmitter in the SC-47 stopped working, so they couldn't contact Wheelus. Maj. Rubertus came up with the idea of having electronics specialist Russell Rafeld switch out the high-frequency transmitter in their SC-47 with the one from the B-24. Although sixteen years had passed since the transmitter was last used, the old radio immediately came to life when power was applied. Sgt. Rafeld was able to contact an airfield near Benghazi to let them know that the SC-47 and L-19 had landed safely at the B-24 crash site. This was just in time to stop the search-and-rescue team from leaving Wheelus to look for them.

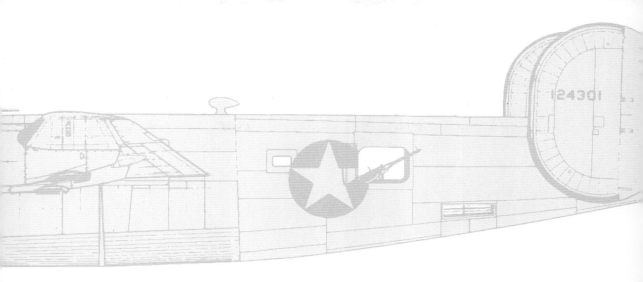

During the examination of the aircraft, it was found that all ten of the .50-caliber machine guns from the B-24 were accounted for and still in working order (other than the chin gun, which had its barrel bent at an 80-degree angle when the plane impacted the desert floor), with almost all their ammunition other than what would be expended to test the guns en route to their target.

Thankfully, somewhere on their flight back to North Africa, the bombload had been dropped; the bomb bay was empty.

The torn-off bomb bay doors and locked-open rear escape hatch indicated that the crew had left the plane by the normal crew escape routes. The open life raft compartments and the missing rafts and emergency equipment puzzled the search team, until it was learned they had been taken earlier by the D'Arcy crew in anticipation of their upcoming leave on the Mediterranean coast, where they could use the rafts. While digging through all the sand on the floor of the nose at the navigator's station, Wes Neep found a map fragment and the navigator's log sheets for the April 4, 1943, mission to Naples. There was a three-hour difference between the takeoff time entered in Navigator Hays's log and official records. This issue was solved by accepting the assumption that Hays, after returning from Cairo before the mission, had used Cairo time in dead-reckoning calculations, one of many mistakes to be found.

The log sheet data and plotted course on the map fragment agreed fully with the briefed route to Naples. However, a blank log sheet after the Lady Be Good turned back at Sorrento raised the nagging questions of why Hays had not continued to determine and plot progress along the return route to Soluch. The sheet referring to the 700-mile return to North Africa contained only a single line of entries: "time, 7:45 pm; course, 140 degrees; altitude, 24,000 feet; speed, 175 mph." One can only speculate why Navigator Hays was unable to do the job he had been trained for during the last six hours that the Lady Be Good remained in the air. The takeoff from Soluch was entered as 1450 local time. Bombardier Woravka's maps of the Naples Harbor area were still on the floor, below his Norden bombsight. The plane's maintenance record (Form 41-B), showing a total of 158 flying hours and listing minor repairs made by its ground crew after arriving in North Africa, was recovered by the D'Arcy exploration party and much later turned over to Wheelus officials. An indication that the Lady Be Good crew actively attempted to orient themselves during the return to Soluch was contained in Radio Operator Robert LaMotte's log, found at his desk.

The single sheet, issued to LaMotte at the mission briefing, listed the plane's call sign as "Faggot 64," along with codes for contacting direction-finding stations along the North African coast and at Malta. Penciled radio transmissions to several of these stations had been added to the sheet by LaMotte during his efforts to get a compass bearing.

One odd find in the aircraft at the flight engineer's station was a thermos containing coffee made on the morning of April 4, 1943. Investigators who tasted some of the coffee deemed it drinkable after sixteen years.

Investigation team has coffee and breakfast in the early morning of May 26. Visible in the photo, *from left to right*, are Capt. John Post, Wesley Neep, A1C James Meadote, Maj. Bill Rubertus, Capt. (Dr.) James Paule, and Lt. Griffen Marr.

The second flight down to the crash site to recover the balance of the L-19 took place a few days after the Fuller/Neep team returned to Wheelus Air Force Base on the coast. The second USAF C-47 (0-3544) taxied up next to the B-24 and parked in preparation for loading the L-19 fuselage in the open clamshell cargo doors of the plane. Because this was an Army plane, US Army mechanics were sent to retrieve it. One such mechanic was Army sergeant Don Venturini, who took photos that day (see page 125).

Early-morning photo taken on the twenty-sixth by US Army photographer Cpl. Gill Hodne. Investigator Neep (*tan hat*) and Maj. Rubertus (*red hat*) stand back near the trailing edge of the left wing, inspecting items from the plane.

CHAPTER 8 THE INSPECTION

Maj. Rubertus walks toward the right side of the aircraft, early morning of the twenty-sixth, to continue the inspection. Note the olive drab paint now visible after sixteen years of wind and sand, wearing some of the desert pink paint off.

CHAPTER 8 THE INSPECTION

Maj. Rubertus stands in front of the #2 engine, examining something on the early morning of May 26. Note the back of the #4 engine sitting in the sand in front of the two left engines.

Maj. Rubertus (*red hat*) and investigator Neep inspect Lady Be Good's #3 propeller on the morning of May 26. Note the chin .50-caliber M2 machine gun, with its barrel bent almost 90 degrees, and the small, carry-around .50-caliber ammo cans thrown out of the nose by the team members.

Close-up of the yet-undamaged dorsal turret Plexiglass dome and the pried-open life raft compartments. Also note that the gas caps on the wings were opened for inspection.

Lady Be Good's tail, showing the break to good advantage, with the C-47 in the background.

Close-up of the left side of Lady Be Good's nose, showing details to good advantage. Most items on the ground were thrown out of the aircraft for inspection by the search team. Note the fire extinguisher that had been removed from the open compartment on the side of the nose.

Left to right: Capt. Myron Fuller, SSgt. Wayne Woods, Col. Henry Elder, and Capt. Rhea Pinkston discuss what they've discovered in the wreckage.

Looking back under the right wing, showing the US national insignia, c. 1943.

In a view from Lady Be Good's nose, note that the debris field is visible stretching out in front of the bomber.

In this view looking from the left side of the cockpit, the #1 engine was visible, bent up at an angle after the crash.

Looking inside the still-undisturbed tail section toward the left waist gun position. The gun hatch is down but not locked. The left waist .50-caliber machine gun is still on its support, with ammo belt and box still in place. The right waist .50-caliber machine gun and its ammo belt are on the floor of the fuselage, along with the round plywood cover that took the place of the ball turret, which was deleted on these particular B-24D models.

CHAPTER 8 THE INSPECTION

Looking inside of the yet-untouched nose, toward the left side, showing the bomb release handles and toggle switches. The object to the left is the "chin" .50-caliber machine gun, which on making contact with the ground was shoved back up inside and jammed up against the left "cheek" .50-caliber machine gun. The barrel of the "chin" gun was bent at almost 90 degrees.

Completely intact tail turret. Over the sixteen years in the desert, the Plexiglass was sandblasted flat. Shortly after the photo was taken, one of the recovery team members broke a section out of the top of the turret to release the intense heat. Note the accumulation of sand that had filtered in to the turret over the sixteen-year period.

Copilot's side of the cockpit, showing the taped control wheel, left armrest, #4 engine throttle lever, and mixture controls.

Center console between the pilot's and copilot's seats, showing the pilot's emergency bomb pull handle (*in red*), landing-gear handle, flap handle, aileron tab, trim wheel, elevator trim wheel, assorted switches, supercharger handles, engine throttle handles, and fuel mixture handles.

Visible in the photo, on the ground next to the left side of the tail section, are all three handheld .50-caliber machine guns mounted in the aft section of the tail, the left and right waist guns, and the "tunnel" gun inserted in a mount in the center of the escape hatch in the belly between the waist guns and the tail turret.

CHAPTER 8 THE INSPECTION

The rear escape hatch opened and locked. This was used by four of Hatton's crew to bail out over the desert at night. Note the socket mount for the "tunnel" gun.

Photo taken the next morning after the team's arrival, showing that the desert pink paint on the left wing had been sandblasted down to the plane's original olive drab paint, as well as the deterioration of the left aileron's fabric covering.

Right side of fuselage, clearly showing the painted word "Good." The "Lady Be" part of the text was crushed on the lower portion of the fuselage. The hand-painted yellow paint has discolored and flaked off.

Nose view the next morning, as the team has coffee and breakfast before delving into the details of the B-24.

Capt. Paule sits in the open dorsal hatch. This photo has been reproduced in many publications, but not to this quality; this was reproduced from the original negative. Note the "chin" .50-caliber machine gun to center left of the photo.

Right side of Lady Be Good's nose, showing the damage done by the crash. Some of the fractured Plexiglass has been removed by the recovery team in order to retrieve some items inside.

Right main landing gear and the #3 engine. Hydraulic fluid has leaked off, letting the gear drop. This also shows the trailing antenna cable wrapped around the prop blade of the #3 engine.

Looking inside the nose after some items had been removed. The left "cheek" .50-caliber machine gun hangs inverted in its socket, with the breech open. The bombardier's seat has been removed from its support, and the back portion of the right "cheek" .50-caliber machine gun is to the left, hanging down.

The back row of cylinders and exhaust collector from the #4 Pratt & Whitney R-1830-43 engine are visible sitting in front of the #1 and #2 engines. After being torn off its mount, it bounced along with Lady Be Good until it came to rest in this position.

One can see that the left wing had virtually no damage from the uncontrolled belly landing. Even the clearance lights on the wingtip were intact.

Looking at the right side of the nose, showing to good advantage the trailing antenna cable wrapped around the #3 prop blade.

Components of Lady Be Good's #4 engine cowling, bomb racks, nosewheel, and engine reduction gear are seen stretched out in front of the aircraft debris field.

Excellent color close-up of the dorsal turret shortly after the investigation team broke a portion of the Plexiglass turret dome to release the intense heat. This shows the .50-caliber machine guns, ammo, and gunsight to good advantage.

Lady Be Good's #4 prop just as it was found, several yards out in front of her nose. Note the white bird waste, where birds have roosted from their futile flight across the desert plateau.

Lady Be Good's nosewheel just as it was found, torn off in the crash in 1943. The team found that when pushed, it rotated freely after sixteen years sitting in the open desert.

Looking toward the nose while the photographer was standing on the right wing root, showing the components torn off Lady Be Good during the crash. Note the #4 props position some 700 feet out; this was the first thing to separate from the aircraft as it rotated through its death slide.

Excellent color photo of the interior of the tail, showing the left waist .50-caliber machine gun and ammo box.

CHAPTER 8 THE INSPECTION

Right "cheek" .50-caliber machine gun still in place.

US Army lieutenant Griffen Marr (pilot of the L-19) confers with A1C James Meadote and Russell Rafeld on the flight down to the crash site discussing how much damage the intense heat did to the engine.

After the determination was made that the L-19's engine was too damaged for the flight back, it was decided to disassemble the aircraft and bring back as many parts as the SC-47 would hold, including the tail assembly, wings, prop, and entire engine cowling assembly. The engine and fuselage would have to be retrieved on the next trip out to the crash site.

Rafeld attempts to remove the engine from the L-19, but the decision was made to leave it for the next flight out. The wings, tail assembly, prop, and engine cowling filled up the SC-47.

Note the yellow stripe painted atop the fuselage. This was done by Wesley Neep so that any other aircraft that overflew Lady Be Good would know that it had already been reported and surveyed.

Air Force A1C James Meadote inspects the tail interior.

One odd find in the aircraft at the flight engineer's station was a thermos containing coffee made on the morning of April 4, 1943. Investigators who tasted some of the coffee deemed it drinkable after sixteen years.

Capt. (Dr.) James Paule sits atop Lady Be Good's dorsal turret prior to the team finishing their investigation.

SC-47 (0-3689) ready to depart the crash site.

Investigator Neep takes one last walk around, inspecting the L-19 to make sure all was secure before departing on the afternoon of May 26, 1959. Note the underside of the right wingtip damage from the crash.

With the L-19 secured under the B-24's tailplane (note the 55-gallon water drum tied to the engine), the investigation team prepares to depart. Though it's hard to see, note the serial number (124301) on the vertical stabilizer.

US Army sergeant Don Venturini took the next seven photographs during the L-19's recovery, three days after the investigation team's departure back to Wheelus.

Sgt. Venturini next to Lady Be Good's nose, May 29, 1959.

US Army aircraft mechanics disassemble the L-19 to load the components into the USAF C-47 (O-3544).

Looking from the nose back toward the broken tail section, you can see that one of the recovery team had removed the headset of copilot Lt. Toner from the copilot's side of the cockpit and hung them on the right-side pitot tube on the nose.

During the L-19 recovery the cockpit enclosure was still intact, but almost half of the dorsal turret dome was broken out; as time went on, all the turret Plexiglass would disappear.

Army mechanic unbolting the L-19's engine for removal, to be hauled into the C-47's open clamshell doors.

Army mechanic does a last inspection before the C-47 departs with the L-19.

One last look inside the cockpit shows that Maj. Bill Rubertus had removed the pilot's control wheel by the time this photo was taken, but left Lt. Hatton's headset just where it had been placed by Hatton sixteen year earlier.

Close-up of the emergency bomb pull handle between the pilot's and copilot's seats.

The black paint faded, part of Lady Be Good's serial number on the left stabilizer, "124301."

CHAPTER 8 THE INSPECTION

CHAPTER 9 ★ THE SEARCH FOR THE CREW

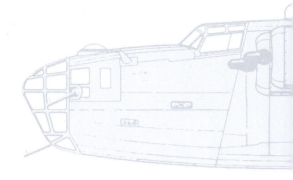

Not long after the joint Army–Air Force visit to the crash site, the discovery of the Lady Be Good was officially reported by Air Force Headquarters in Wiesbaden, Germany, then to American wire services. The Associated Press issued the following release on June 4, 1959: "A special team of investigators has been charged with investigating the wartime crash of an American Liberator bomber in the Libyan Desert sixteen years ago, the US Air Force reported today." It said the discovery of an American four-engine bomber in the trackless wastes had presented one of the greatest mysteries of modern times. The story was immediately picked up by nearly every daily newspaper in America, as well as the rest of the world.

At this time, Fuller and Neep drew up detailed planes to search the desert surrounding the Lady Be Good. They were told by desert survival experts that Lt. Hatton and his crew's remains shouldn't be very far from the B-24, considering that three of the engines had run out of fuel and shut down with the props feathered not long before the crew bailed out. Neep and Fuller had plans laid out for a grid search with vehicles that were made specifically for desert operations.

Arrangements were made to add Fuller and Neep's team to Saly & Co. Ltd., a salvage and mine clearance firm that at that time was ready to embark on a salvage operation out across the Sand Sea of Calanscio to traverse the flat desert plateau to its east. Medical supplies, signaling equipment, water, gasoline, and radios all were needed and procured from the US Air Force and Army Engineer Detachment, then delivered to Wheelus base operations to be flown to the crash site. An Air Force C-47 supply aircraft was scheduled to land near the B-24 on June 10 to meet up with and resupply the search team; that is, if everything went as planned. The Saly & Co. expedition left Benghazi early on June 5; vehicles consisted of one Land Rover, one Dodge Power Wagon, a Dodge 6 × 6 weapons carrier, and a large Bedford truck. Personnel in the convoy were Alexander Karadzic, a former Royal Air Force navigator and desert survival expert; Capt. Myron Fuller; investigator Wesley Neep; and a Libyan police chief (Rahil), who knew the area to be crossed and the Libyan drivers and mechanics (as will be remembered, at this time only Libyan nationals were sanctioned to drive in Libya).

Two days out, the Bedford truck was left at the Pump House Ruins, with its extra fuel and water to be picked up and used on their return trip. Traversing the Kufra Trail, a caravan route connecting the Kufra Oasis with the Libyan coast at 450 miles south, they turned east and left the trail, entering the Sand Sea of Calanscio Dunes on June 7, with the surface getting softer and softer, which made it difficult to make any

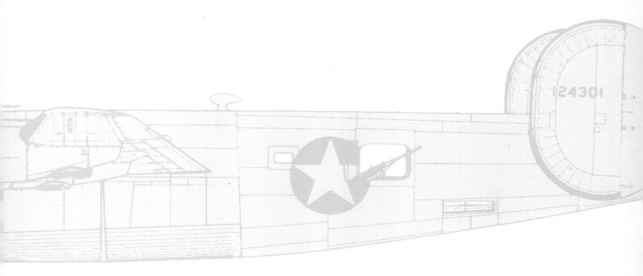

respectable distance with the trucks constantly getting bogged down. The police chief indicated that a passage across the dunes would be found. As the high-crested dunes rose in elevation, the men were constantly having a hard time making progress.

To be able to get any traction in the dunes once they had dug in up to the bottom of the rims, PSP (pierced steel planking) steel plates had to be wedged under the wheels. As the crow flies in a straight line, the Sand Sea was only 60 miles across to the flat, hard-surface plateau. Due to the many passages that had to be found through the dunes, which rose from 50 to 500 feet in elevation, the vehicles had to drive over 90 miles crossing the dunes to get to the gravel plateau, which could put the caravan behind schedule with the C-47 supply aircraft at the crash site. By the third day in the dunes, Capt. Fuller, Alexander Karadzic, and Rahil decided to go ahead with the Land Rover to make sure they met the C-47, carrying the much-needed fuel and water, at noon on June 10; they just made it before the arrival time of the supply aircraft. Three hours later, the rest of the caravan made it through the San Sea in 130-degree heat to the crash site, almost out of water. Rendezvous with the supply aircraft was planned to be at 1200, but the aircraft didn't show up until almost 1600, circled several times for almost an hour with its landing gear down, then flew off north toward its base. With no radio communication with the plane, and because water was running low for the entire group, it was decided to send one truck with empty 55-gallon water drums to a watering hole on a 300-mile round trip.

The following afternoon, the C-47 was again overhead, and this time it landed. It was found out that the day before, the aircraft had a warning light on the instrument panel, showing that the landing gear was down but not locked in place. On their return to Wheelus AFB, they put the gear down again, and with the warning light still on, they made an emergency landing, expecting the gear to collapse, but there was never anything wrong with the gear; it was just a bad instrument light.

The gravel plain surrounding the Lady Be Good covers over 18,000 square miles. Thinking that the crew had deduced that they were southeast of their base and would head northwest, the men still had more than 8,000 square miles that might have to be searched. It was very important to find the bailout point and use that to start the search from.

Using this plan, the men searched an area of 450 square miles, with the B-24 as the center point, during the first six days, hoping to find the rally point after bailout. Nothing was found by then, so it was decided to move the search north and west on the basis of the idea that the crew would have started walking on the 330-degree compass heading, the opposite of the course flown by the B-24 returning from Sorrento.

The Libyan guide estimated that even if each of the crew members had a half canteen of water, they couldn't last much more than 35 miles, which was the limit the crew could walk in the 130-degree-plus temperature during the day. It was thought that the men, weakened from dehydration, would have died in a group.

On June 16, while following the northwest track, the search team spotted a pair of sheepskin-lined flight boots oriented along the 330-degree course heading. This was just 19 miles north of the Lady Be Good crash site.

The following morning, on June 17, a 39-square-mile area was searched, using the boots as the center, but nothing was found. In making more sweeps to the north, the team made a discovery of the wheel tracks of five large trucks that had passed heading north of the boots, oriented along a 340-to-342-degree compass heading. It was speculated that these tracks were made by World War II vehicles that had passed through the area at least a year before the Lady Be Good had crashed. The five sets of tracks all were made by the same type of vehicles, the Italian Lancia diesel trucks that had retreated from the 1941 French attack on the Kufra Oasis. Hatton and his crew had come across them during their walk northwest and made a decision to follow the tracks, thinking it would possibly lead to water. It was decided by the search team to follow the Italian tracks north.

On June 19, with two of the search teams' vehicles following the tracks north, one vehicle drove directly on the tracks while the second drove alongside the tracks, a quarter of a mile to the east. About 2 miles from where the vehicles started up the tracks, an arrowhead-shaped marker made from a parachute, a pair of flight boots, and a pile of cut parachute shroud lines was located. A mile and a half farther up the trail was a complete inner liner from an electrically heated flying suit. A few hundred feet beyond were two parachutes. One, pointing north, was cut to form an arrowhead, held down with small stones, visible mainly because of the pattern made by the stones. The second parachute was rolled up and positioned at the foot of the arrowhead, under a section of parachute harness with the name "V. L. Moore" stenciled on it. Moore was one of Lt. Hatton's men.

More parachute markers and assorted pieces of flight gear were found heading up the Italian tracks for the next 15 miles, with a total so far of six parachute markers forming arrowheads pointing north along the tracks. Not far past the sixth marker, the tracks intersected a mile-wide trail made by some seventy-five to eighty vehicles on a compass heading of 20 degrees. It was later found out that after following this trail for 35 miles, the crew had found several British 4-imperial-gallon gas cans scattered along the trail, indicating that these tracks were made by the British Long Range Desert Group when they had moved its headquarters from Siwa Oasis to Kufra, a year before the Lady Be Good crash-landed.

The intersection of the two trails going in different directions would have required a tough decision by Hatton and his men. After the effort the crew made to mark their direction of travel, to the search team it looked like Hatton and crew decided to stay on their original course following the Italian tracks to find help. There was a large amount of drifting sand that had covered most of the intersection of the two different tracks, which also may have covered any markers left by the crew, so the search team followed both tracks for 35 miles each but found that the tracks faded out the nearer they got to the dunes to the north. It was then decided after conferring with the police chief and utilizing his knowledge of survival in this region that the crew's remains would be found somewhere northwest, in an area somewhere between the two vehicle tracks but before the crew would have reached the dunes to the north.

This next phase of the search would be far too much for the team and the two vehicles, which were starting to break down, requiring at least thirty more days of intensive activity plus the use of helicopters, so it was decided to terminate this part of the search, return to the Lady Be Good, and plan for the next part of the mission. An Air Force C-47 from Benghazi was sent down to the B-24 crash site to pick up Neep and Fuller, arriving on June 22. Saly & Co. left for the coast the following day and returned five days later, on the twenty-seventh.

In the second phase of the search, Wes Neep and Capt. Fuller, together with officials from Saly & Co., flew to Tripoli to talk to the commanding officer of the 329th Engineer Detachment. A plan was devised by Fuller and Neep to add helicopters to the search area, but the plans were shelved because of mechanical problems, so they fell back on an alternate plan of using not only more, but better-equipped ground vehicles—again supplied by the Saly company.

On July 3, the Frankfurt mortuary search team returned to Benghazi to make final preparations for the second phase of the search for the Lady Be Good crew. For this expedition, Saly & Co. provided a large Italian Lancia truck capable of carrying forty drums of gasoline, water, and oil. For general purpose, Dodge Power Wagons carrying additional fuel, water, food, and camp equipment were added. Two Land Rovers were to be used for scouting in the dune areas.

Leaving Benghazi on July 10, the motorized convoy took seven days to reach a site 380 miles southeast of Benghazi, where they set up camp from which to do a detailed search of approximately 1,000 square miles along the 50-mile marked trail left by the crewmen sixteen years previous. On July 17, Gen. H. R. Spicer, commander of the 17th Air Force, based at Tripoli, landed near the Lady Be Good site and was met by a motor convoy from the camp site located 50 miles north.

Gen. Spicer had been following this story since the Lady Be Good's discovery and had been intently interested in what had happened to the crew. The general himself just sixteen years before had fought during the war as a full-bird colonel, flying P-51 Mustangs with the 357th Fighter Group. On one of his strafing missions, he had been shot down by ground fire over France, where he bailed out and was taken prisoner by the SS. As the ranking officer in his prisoner-of-war camp, he defied the Luftwaffe camp commander when he was instructed to tell his men never to try to break out of the camp; because of this, the Germans said they would make an example out of him and execute him in front of the entire camp, but before this happened, the Soviet Red Army overran the camp. Spicer was a man loved and respected not only by all who served with and under him, but by the entire POW camp he was held prisoner in.

On July 19, a special team was put together to penetrate the dunes, following the five Italian vehicle tracks. Gen. Spicer came with the team, wanting to know what they might discover. They covered 51 miles into the dunes and 164 straight-line air miles from the Lady Be Good site in two and a half days, with the tracks disappearing in the shifting sand. They then returned to their starting point and did the same thing on the British tracks, until they too disappeared into the dunes.

On July 20, Gen. Spicer's radio operator was driven back to the general's C-47, near the B-24, to call Wheelus AFB. On their way back to base camp, taking a little bit of a different route, they made the accidental discovery of a seventh parachute marker over 60 feet east of the Italian tracks. This parachute, in shredded tatters but still in an arrowhead shape, as held down by the small stones for over sixteen years, was pointing at 325 degrees, which lined up with all the previous markers. The search teams now concentrated on the four grid squares covering 400 square miles north of the last markers and intersecting trails. The intense heat of July in the Sahara was starting to get to the vehicles, with breakdowns plaguing the team, so Fuller and Neep asked the general if he could expedite some helicopters out to the crash site to help in the search. With no remains of the crew being found thus far, on July 21, Spicer said he would take care of it, then boarded his plane and returned to Wheelus AFB to get that started.

The Pentagon granted permission for the use of helicopters to be brought down by two C-130s from their base at Evreau, France, along with a new convoy of trucks from Benghazi loaded with supplies, which drove down 440 miles to the crash site.

During the wait for the helicopters, the search team continued out across the plateau along the marked trail of parachute markers that Hatton and his crew had left, starting 18 miles north of the crash site and running the edge of the Calanscio Sand Sea.

The lead vehicle had a sun compass laid out on the truck's hood. This was a horizontal dial with azimuth markings and a vertical needle in the center, which casts a shadow from the sun on the dial. The driver and crew of this vehicle first take a conventional compass heading along the course to be searched, then follow the reading by driving straight ahead and keeping the sun-shadow reading constant. The second vehicle follows the first and makes zigzag sweeps along either side of the first vehicle's course. In this way, anything on the surface will be spotted.

On July 23, during the search of the wide intersection of the Italian and British vehicle tracks, a section of parachute harness was found pointing on a 325–145-degree axis; then, 425 yards in the direction the harness was pointing, they found a leather flight helmet, and 175 yards farther they found knotted sections of shroud line. These markers were all lying in the wide intersection of the 340- and 20-degree trails.

This led the search team to believe that Hatton and his crew had decided to change course to the new 325-degree heading, possibly thinking this new heading was the opposite direction of their flight path down into the desert. The search team also found that both the Italian and British truck trails had faded out from blowing sand some 35 miles farther north.

Multiple breakdowns of the search vehicles were becoming a major problem because of the extreme heat, which made it clear that the helicopters were needed as soon as possible to overfly the terrain leading up to and over the Sand Sea. There was also a question as to where to store the incoming fuel for the search vehicles, when someone suggested using the B-24's fuel tanks. It was found on the first trip to the Lady Be Good that the self-sealing rubber fuel cells lining the bombers tanks were still in good condition. When Maj. Rubertus removed the caps from three of the tanks on top of the wings, the sound of inrushing air was heard, so it was thought that there was no damage to the tanks in the crash sixteen years earlier. Because of this discovery, 390 gallons of fuel was pumped into one of the B-24 wing tanks. The balance of the incoming gas was put in two drums. However, the exposure to sixteen years of the extreme desert heat had weakened the integrity of the bladder tanks, and all the transferred fuel leaked out and soaked into the sand during the night.

At 0625 on August 16, 1959, C-130A, serial number 57-0459, of the 39th Troop Carrier Squadron (TCS), based at Evreau, France, lifted off from the runway at Berka outside Benghazi, Libya, and headed southeast. Their destination was almost 450 miles south, to one of the most desolate and isolated places on the face of the earth, to land near the derelict bomber.

At the controls was Capt. Sheldon (Shelly) McConnell, United States Air Force, an expert multiple-engine pilot who had been involved in many low-level combat missions in all types of weather flying B-25Js in Italy during the Second World War. But nothing prepared him for the landing he would make just fifteen years later in a Lockheed C-130A on the Calanscio Plateau, deep inside the Libyan desert. This was the first large resupply mission for the search team on the ground looking for the crew of the Lady Be Good.

Capt. McConnell's aircraft was at the time (1959) a very new and innovative aerial military cargo hauler. C-130s could operate from unimproved short dirt airstrips, but this was going to be put to the test.

McConnell's aircraft was loaded with two disassembled Hiller H-23 helicopters from the 329th Army Engineering Detachment, a 4 × 4 survey vehicle from Saly & Co., the Army flight crew for the H-23s, and a Hiller Aircraft technical representative to supervise their reassembly and to verify how they would operate under special desert conditions. The temperatures in that region in August reached upward of 130 degrees. This would also be a test for the new little helicopters. No. 459 also was carrying an APU for subsequent C-130 trips to Lady Be Good's crash site; needless to say, a full load.

The plan was to fly down to the site; offload the helicopters, personnel, and equipment; fly back to Berka to reload with fuel, water, and supplies for the vehicles, helicopters, and search team; and fly back to the site the next day in preparation for the combined air ground search for the B-24's crew.

There was no runway, of course, just this huge, flat expanse of sand and gravel surrounded by large sand dunes. There had been trips made to the crash site by C-47s since the previous May, but this was the first time an aircraft the size and weight of a C-130 would attempt to land on the plateau. At 76,780 pounds empty, a maximum gross weight of 155,000 pounds, and her low belly just inches from the ground, there was some concern on just how far she would sink into the desert sand.

The flight down at 25,000 feet was uneventful, until McConnell arrived over the Lady Be Good and descended. The Army search team, headed by Capt. Myron Fuller and forensics investigator Wes Neep, had already made the trek to the crash site some days before in desert vehicles and were busy lighting smoke flares to give the C-130 the wind direction on the ground.

McConnell dropped down to 1,500 feet and made a pass down the landing area to get the desired heading a few hundred yards behind the Liberator. After turning and dropping lower, what he and his copilot saw out of the windscreen was a bright, shimmering, blurred horizon caused by the heat waves, which gave them the feeling of landing uphill.

There weren't any sharp reference points on the ground in front of them, only the blurred, curved horizon. This caused a disconcerting vertigo with both pilots, but Capt. McConnell remembered back to the report he read from the first aircraft to land out here back on May 25, a C-47 piloted by Maj. Bill Rubertus.

His first thoughts were "I can't tell weather I'm 50 or 500 feet off the ground!" McConnell immediately went to an instrument landing, indicating this to his copilot, 1Lt. Harry S. Thompson; their eyes both went to the gauges and instruments.

With 50 percent flaps and the radio altimeter set at 1,000 feet, they turned downwind. When the landing site appeared to be about 45 degrees back of the wingtips, he set 500 feet into the radio altimeter and turned on base leg, descending to this altitude. Upon turning final, he set the radio altimeter to 25 feet and set his descent up with 100 percent flaps to make his touchdown at the desired point. Establishing computed flare speed for 100 percent flaps just prior to reaching 25 feet and as the red light came on, he retarded power and established his landing altitude. The navigator, sitting behind the copilot, called out the altitude indicated on the radio altimeter on final approach at intervals. And finally, McConnell told Lt. Thompson to look down out his side window and tap his shoulder when he could see pebbles on the ground rushing up to them. As the navigator counted down to the last few feet, Lt. Thompson tapped on Shelly's shoulder, and at that, Shelly cut power to the throttles, flared, and touched down without so much as even a small jolt. As 459 rolled out, McConnell felt the steering in the nosewheel as very positive, with very little drag from what he expected on the sandy desert surface. Shelly and his crew flashed each other big grins and nods. "Piece of cake!" quipped Lt. Thompson.

McConnell increased the throttles to taxi around, turning the nosewheel easily so that they would come back in the direction they had landed, and came to a stop a few hundred yards behind the Lady Be Good.

After shutting down the engines and securing the aircraft, the flight crew piled out the access door and onto the desert floor. Capt. McConnell looked back at the plane and the tracks the landing gear had made, and was amazed. This aircraft, with a full load of helicopters, a truck, an APU, and personnel, had landed in the open desert on a desolate plateau and had sunk into the sand by only 2 inches!

While the H-23's flight crew and other personnel were busy offloading the equipment and helicopters, McConnell and his crew inspected the famed B-24 for themselves.

Marveling at her excellent condition after sixteen years in the desert, Shelly commented to Lt. Thompson that if there had been someone at her controls, she could have made a successful wheels-down landing with no problems. If the #4 engine had also been shut down with a feathered prop like #1, #2, and #3, she would have bellied in in a straight line instead of sliding in an arc from the torque of the #4 engine running at full throttle, and probably would not have broken her back—a lot of "what ifs?"

After the equipment was unloaded and a short meal, it was time for the C-130 to head back to Benghazi to reload all the supplies, fuel, and water that the search team would need, then fly back the next day.

After takeoff and level-out at 20,000 feet, Shelly put 459 on autopilot for the return trip and reached back behind his seat for an olive drab bag. Lt. Thompson asked, "What do you have there, captain?" Shelly grinned and reached in to pull out several items. McConnell said, "Just a few things I 'liberated' from the Liberator!" But it seemed that just about everybody came away with something that day.

The items included the red emergency "BOMB PULL" handle that was located behind the center console between the pilot's and copilot's seats, the Bakelite handles and trigger mechanism for the twin .50-caliber tail turret guns, a throat mike found wedged down between the left side of pilot's seat and the fuselage (undoubtedly belonging to Lt. Hatton, the Lady Be Good's pilot), and an emergency signal mirror still in its paper case. Prior to moving to the Air Force Village in Colorado Springs from Hemet, California, in 1993, retired colonel Sheldon McConnell was kind enough to give the author all of these prized items, which in the future will be donated to a worthy aviation museum.

Two days after the C-130 departed, the two Hillers and all the equipment were moved to Camp No. 2, north of the crash site, and were prepared for the continued ground as well as air search. An eighth parachute was found a mile and a half east and slightly south of the first flight boots, but it wasn't laid out in an arrowhead like the others; it was rolled up and left next to the 340-degree trail. The eighth parachute had the search team thinking that all of the crew had jumped together, and that this might be the last marker they would find.

They based this on what they thought were complete parachutes to make each of the arrowheads found pointing north up the 340-degree Italian tracks. It was later found that the crew saved the chutes by cutting strips from the silk to make the markers instead of using each entire parachute for the arrowheads; this saved material for several more arrowhead markers. Grid searches were set up and flown by the two helicopters flying a mile apart, sweeping back and forth, each with an observer, and covering 2-square-mile perimeters outlined by wheel tracks from two trucks. When each grid square was covered by the helicopters, they would move north to the next grid. During this search, when the helicopters were some 18 miles from Camp No. 2, they spotted some bleached-white bones below. After landing to investigate, they discovered the skeletal remains of four large camels along with cooking utensils and other items. A search of the surrounding area yielded one more skeleton, but this one was human. By examination of the bones and the cooking utensils, it was determined that this caravan had perished at least 100–200 years before. The investigation now indicated that the crew had followed the World War II tracks north into the dunes and died somewhere in the Sand Sea.

After finding the camel caravan and ascertaining the age of the skeletal remains, Neep and Fuller thought that if Hatton and his crew had perished on the gravel plain, the search team would have found their remains by this time. Sweeps continued until they had flown over 15 miles into the Sand Sea, but they found nothing.

By August 31, after several intrusions by the helicopters with their support vehicles into the labyrinth of the southern end of the Calanscio sand dunes, some almost 500 feet high, the search for Hatton and his crew, for now, came to a close. Camp No. 2 was dismantled and relocated back to the Lady Be Good.

Two weeks after arriving with the helicopters, a C-130 flew down to the crash site to load up the two Hillers and their crews along with both Capt. Fuller and investigator Neep, to be brought back to Benghazi. The balance of the search team and their vehicles returned on the route they had come down on. After a three-day rest at Wheelus, Capt. Fuller and Wes Neep laid out the details of the search to Army and Air Force officials and the US press corps on what the search revealed. The next day they both flew back to their headquarters in Frankfurt, Germany, to document their operations in the desert. On the basis of all their findings, in their final report Neep and Fuller concluded that "The crew had perished in the sand dunes and had been covered over by the sands." Thus officially ended the desert search—or so they thought.

Photo showing to good advantage how the vehicles were constantly getting bogged down in the soft sand while crossing the dunes.

US Army Air Force high-altitude sheepskin flight boots discovered 19 miles north of the Lady Be Good crash site.

June 19, 1959: the discovery of the outline of a parachute marker held down by stones, placed by Lady Be Good's crew in 1943.

Investigation team's vehicles skirting the Sand Sea to the west while following the Italian truck tracks.

Capt. Fuller and Gen. Spicer examine the right nose .50-caliber machine gun after it had been removed from its position in the nose.

Standing in front of Lady Be Good's #4 engine mount, Capt. Fuller and Gen. Spicer examine an old camel saddle found in the desert during the search for the crew.

Sun compass laid out on the hood of the search vehicle.

US Army captain Myron C. Fuller and the Saly Oil Co. Land Rover.

CHAPTER 9 THE SEARCH FOR THE CREW

Air Force and Army personnel discover a seventh parachute marker by accident off the original track that the team was following.

CHAPTER 9 THE SEARCH FOR THE CREW

Search vehicles traversing the plateau near the Sand Sea.

Shifting dunes west of the plateau.

Libyan drivers for the Saly Oil Co. with investigator Wes Neep, who wisely covers his head from the brutal sun.

The first USAF C-130A flown by Capt. Shelly McConnell to land near the Lady Be Good crash site. Note that the heavily loaded aircraft sank only a few inches into the sand surface.

In a view looking back between Lady Be Good's #1 and #2 engines (and what's left of #4 engine), the C-130 unloads her cargo: an APU unit, two Hiller H-23 helicopters, and a Saly Oil Co. truck.

CHAPTER 9 THE SEARCH FOR THE CREW

C-130A USAF 70459 busy unloading its cargo near the B-24 wreck.

Capt. McConnell next to the Lady Be Good's wing.

Capt. Sheldon McConnell posing between the twin .50-caliber machine guns in the Lady Be Good's dorsal turret; as can be seen, the entire Plexiglass turret dome was gone by this time.

459 during unloading of the supplies and helicopters; note that the moon is visible.

Plexiglass on top of the Consolidated tail turret had been all but completely broken out for access, and to release the intense heat that built up during the day.

Tail section of the B-24, showing the rotted rudder fabric to good advantage.

Tail of Capt. McConnell's C-130A behind the B-24.

Capt. Fuller and Lt. Thompson have a short conference before Thompson and Capt. McConnell depart.

After assembly, the Hiller H-23s were up and running the next morning in preparation for flight to Camp #2.

CHAPTER 9 THE SEARCH FOR THE CREW

Emergency bomb pull handle from the Lady Be Good.

Bakelite firing handles for the Lady Be Good's Consolidated A6A tail turret.

Lt. Hatton's USAAF throat mic, found wedged down between the pilot's seat and left bulkhead.

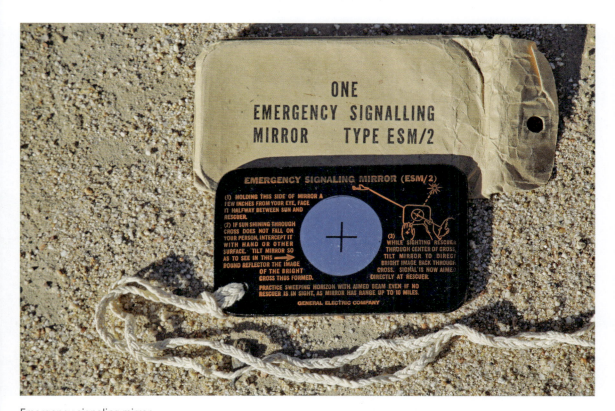

Emergency signaling mirror.

The trackless towering sand dunes of the Sand Sea of Calanscio.

Lt. Tom Gochner was the US Army pilot who flew Wes Neep in his H-23 search helicopter, looking for the lost crewmen.

CHAPTER 9 THE SEARCH FOR THE CREW

CHAPTER 10 ★ THE DISCOVERY OF FIVE CREW REMAINS

Press releases on the Lady's lost crew attracted the attention of Americans across the country. It also got a television producer, Robert E. Costello, involved. Working through the Department of Defense, Costello flew to Wheelus Air Force Base with scriptwriter Roger Hirson and Maj. Paul Fallon, the latter of whom had flown on the April 4, 1943, mission and was also friends with (and had taken flight training with) Bill Hatton. The men discussed the bomber and her missing crew with Maj. Bill Rubertus and press officer Walt Wandell. After a lengthy discussion, Maj. Rubertus flew the group down to the B-24 crash site on October 31, 1959.

In February 1960, Costello produced the Armstrong Circle Theater live television documentary telling the story of the Lady Be Good and its crew. Included in the live broadcast was Col. Norman Appold, squadron operations officer of the 376th Bomb Group on April 4, 1943; and Maj. William Rubertus, who had made the first official USAF flight to the crash site and several subsequent flights.

BP exploration teams continued to look for oil throughout the Calanscio Plateau and surrounding ocean of dunes. Support for the oil company operations was airlifted from Benghazi by Douglas C-47s operated by Silver City Airlines. Capt. Oldrich Dolezal, a former Royal Air Force pilot during World War II, was one of the pilots flying for Silver City in 1960. On February 11, 1960, he landed his C-47 next to one of the BP oil exploration parties working along the southern edge of the Sand Sea of Calanscio.

This British Petroleum team was led by American geologist James Backhaus, whose team was gathering seismic data from subsurface rock strata near the dunes on the edge of the gravel plain. This area was approximately 85 miles northwest of the B-24 crash site. A few days before, Capt. Dolezal landed with his supplies for the camp, and while crossing a wide valley between two long fingers of dunes coming from the Sand Sea to the north, one of Backhaus's exploration teams discovered the half-covered skeletal remains of five humans, all close together. Anyone connected with BP's oil exploration in Libya in 1959 knew about the search operations for the crew of the World War II bomber. Backhaus's exploration team had no doubt about what they had stumbled across: five of the Lady Be Good's crew.

Backhaus gave the coordinates of the five remains to Capt. Dolezal (27°50'N, 23°34'E) prior to him flying back to base, and asked him to call Wheelus Air Base on the radio after taking off. Dolezal radioed the control tower at the commercial airport in Tripoli, relaying the information of the find; this in turn was passed along to the USAF at Wheelus Base. Col. Stebbins Griffith, who commanded the base, was immediately informed.

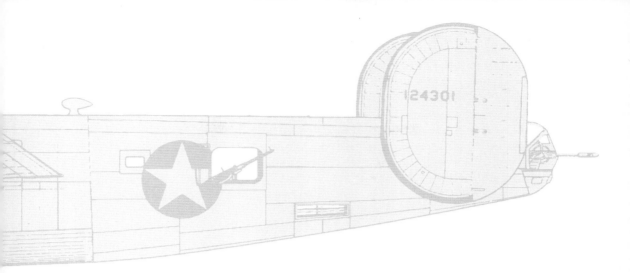

    Col. Griffith had scheduled a barbecue for several of the base officers; included was Maj. Bill Rubertus, who was the pilot of the first USAF team down to the Lady Be Good's crash site. Griffith told Rubertus about the discovery of the five remains and said to have a plane ready for an early-morning takeoff to the location of the BP camp.

    Col. Griffith had the forethought to bring an Air Force chaplain, William Woods; Air Force information officer Walter Wandell; USAF photographers; and Capt. Dolezal to help with the navigation to the BP camp. Maj. Rubertus had just returned from the Armstrong Circle Theater television broadcast, which was aired on February 2, and was slated to fly as copilot with Col. Griffith as the SC-47 pilot.

    On February 12, with Griffith at the controls, the SC-47 took off heading south into the desert. The flight to the survey camp had no problems until the landing. It turns out that Griffith experienced the same thing Capt. Shelly McConnell did when he piloted the first C-130A to the B-24 crash site; the horizon blended with the desert floor from the shimmering heat effect, blurring everything in front of them. Griffith turned to copilot Rubertus and said, "Damn, I can't tell if I'm 50 or 500 feet off the ground!"

    Maj. Rubertus had also experienced the same feeling of vertigo on his first visit to the B-24. He told Griffith to make an instrument approach to the landing and to keep his eyes on the cockpit gauges. The SC-47 made the approach and touched down with a perfect three-point landing with barely a notice.

    BP had the trucks to get the flight crew and passengers from the camp to the edge of the Sand Sea, out to the location of the five remains. Hatton and his men *had* left the 340-degree trail of the five Italian vehicles and switched to the 325-degree heading. This took them between two massive sand dune fingers projecting out onto the gravel plain, which stretched over 15 miles across from one dune finger to the other. They were over halfway up in between these dune fingers when they couldn't walk or stand anymore; this was over 75 miles from where they had landed in the desert after bailing out at 0200. They may have lasted another night and into the next day before taking their last breath and dying, grouped a few feet from each other. Col. Griffith and his group examined the dog tags of the remains, identifying some of them on the spot. Some of the items scattered around the bodies were two empty canteens standing next to each other, and a portion of a silk parachute that had covered the last ones alive, to try to protect them from the bitter cold at night and the blistering heat by day,

    Griffith flew everyone back to Wheelus that afternoon, then contacted the Army, asking that the mortuary team from Frankfurt, Germany, be sent back down to recover the crew's remains. Capt. Myron Fuller, who knew that part of the desert quite well from the year before, was chosen to direct the recovery operations.

Investigator Wes Neep was also requested but was unavailable and out of Europe at the time on another case, so investigator Hugo Schaeffer accompanied Fuller.

On February 17, Benjamin Lambeth, the deputy commander at Wheelus, flew Fuller and Schaeffer out to the five remains to start their detailed recovery of the bodies and personal effects. Some of what they found were two canteens, a lieutenant's overseas cap, silk survival maps of the area, a British-issue survival kit, a flashlight, a rolled-up life preserver, several pairs of shoes, and a Red Cross sweater. There was also a yellow Mae West life vest, saved by one of the crew, who was probably thinking if they found water to the north, they could fill the vest along with the canteens. Clothing from the men who had died first were used by the ones still living to help keep a little warmer during the freezing nights.

Fuller and Schaeffer were surprised at the condition of the bodies, especially the mummification that took place below the surface of the sand. The floor of the flat gravel plain prior to entering the dunes was free of any blowing sand until the surface was disturbed and the underlying fine sand was exposed to the wind. The last movements of the five men at the site had broken the thin surface, exposing the silty fine sand beneath their bodies, which, after some time had passed, covered portions of them with loose sand. Any of the men's bodies that were above the level of the sand had been eroded down to bare skeletons.

During the examination of the crew's clothing, Capt. Fuller found a small pocket diary with a leather name tag, on which was written "Lt. R. F. Toner," Hatton's copilot. The first entry was March 2, 1943, at Morrison Field, Florida, and the entries ended on April 12, 1943.

These are the entries in Lt. Toner's diary, starting on the day they took off from their base on the coast of Libya for their first, and what turned out to be their last, mission:

Sunday, April 4, 1943: Naples–28 planes. Things pretty well mixed up. Got lost returning, out of gas, jumped, landed in desert at 2:00 in morning. No one badly hurt. Can't find John [Woravka]. All others present.

Monday, 5th: Start walking N.W. Still no John. A few rations, ½ canteen of water, 1 capful per day. Sun fairly warm. Good breeze from N.W. Nites very cold, no sleep. Rested and walked.

Tuesday, 6th: Rested at 11:30. Sun very warm, no breeze. Spent p.m. in hell. No planes, etc. Rested until 5:00 p.m. Walked and rested all nite, 15 minutes on, 5 off.

Wednesday, 7th: Same routine. Everyone getting weak. Can't get very far. Prayers all the time. Again, p.m. very warm hell. Can't sleep. Everyone sore from ground.

Thursday, 8th: Hit sand dunes. Very miserable. Good wind but continuous blowing of sand. Everyone now very weak. Thought Sam and Moor were all done. LaMotte eyes are gone. Everyone else's eyes are bad. Still going N.W.

Friday, 9th: Shelley, Rip, Moore separate and try to go for help. Rest of us all very weak, eyes bad. Not any travel. All want to die. Still very little water. Nites are about 35 degrees. Good N. wind. No shelter, 1 parachute left.

Saturday, 10th: Still having prayer meetings for help. No signs of anything, a couple of birds. Good wind from N. Really weak now, can't walk. Pains all over. Still all want to die. Nites very cold. No sleep.

Sunday, 11th: Still waiting for help. Still praying. Eyes bad. Lost all our weight. Aching all over. Could make it if we had water. Just enough left to put our tongue to. Have hope for help very soon. No rest. Still same place.

Monday, 12th: No help yet. Very cold nite.

The investigators arrived at the site of the five crewmen's remains on February 17, 1960. The drawing on page 165 shows the position of the remains before exhumation, and the position of each piece of clothing and equipment that was found on the surface. All five remains were partially covered with fine sand; everything above ground was a skeleton. After the bodies were removed, it could be seen that all unexposed portions below the surface were completely mummified.

Recovery operations began on February 18, 1960, and revealed the following:

Unknown X-1 was identified as 1st Lt. William J Hatton, on basis of two identification tags around neck and tooth chart comparison. Remains had no clothses on and in an extended prone position.

Unknown X-2 was identified as 2nd Lt. D. P. Hayes on the basis of tooth chart comparison and presence of USAAF Navigator ring on middle finger of right hand. With exception of suntan trousers, no other clothing was found on remains. Deceased was lying extended on back.

Unknown X-3 was identified as SSgt. Samuel E. Adams on the basis of two identification tags around neck and tooth chart comparison. Remains had no clothes on and lying partially on his back.

Unknown X-4 was identified as TSgt. Robert E. LaMotte on the basis of one identification tag around neck and tooth chart comparison. Remains had no clothes on and lying on left side.

Unknown X-5 was identified as 2nd Lt. Robert F. Toner, on basis of name plate on flying jacket found on remains, also several pieces of clothing belonging to the deceased were recovered in close proximity. Entries in the diary found eliminated the possibility of those remains being any of the four still missing crewmembers. Tooth chart comparison could not be made at the site due to the mummified condition of facial area. Two flight jackets were found on the remains, one wrapped around legs had no markings, the position of the second jacket with leather tab "Robert F. Toner" indicated deceased was either removing or putting on jacket as left arm was in the sleeve and the right was out of sleeve. Deceased was lying on right side.

Remains were placed in human remains pouches and upon return to Wheelus AFB, and were placed in transfer cases for flight to Frankfurt, Germany.

MYRON C. FULLER JR.
Capt. QMC
Asst. Adjutant

HUGO A. SCHAFFER
US DAC Field Investigator

CONDITION OF THE BODIES OF THE FIRST FIVE CREW MEMBERS

1. The discovery of five (5) bodies of USAAF crewmembers in the Libyan Desert, some 355 miles S/E of Benghazi, had resulted in their recovery and association with missing members of the aircrew which parachuted the night of 4/5 April 1943 from B-24 bomber aircraft No. 41-24301. Identification tags, rings, dental comparisons and clothing markings have identified the group as the following personnel:

1Lt.	William J. Hatton
2Lt.	D. P. Hays
2Lt.	Robert F. Toner
TSgt.	Robert E. La Motte
SSgt.	Samuel E. Adams

2. Each remains was found partially covered by the drifting sand, and the exposed areas of each body were eroded and bleached white from the driven sand and intense sunlight. The unexposed areas of the bodies were protected by the sand and become mummified. Teeth exposed to the sun became very brittle and were cracked and splintered into fine fragments. The protected teeth were in a state of perfect preservation. Unexposed head hair was found to agree with the recorded hair colors for each of the above listed crewmen while the exposed portions of the hair was bleached to a light blond.

Lt. William J. Hatton
This body was complete, intact and was found lying face down in an extended position. The teeth were negative for all associated crewmembers except Lt. HATTON and Sgt ADAMS. It is noted that similar teeth in case X-70110 have been definitely associated as those of Sgt. ADAMS. Two (2) identification tags for WILLIAM J HATTON were found suspended from the neck by a plastic cord along with two (2) religious medals. The religious medals coincide with the Catholic faith recorded for Lt. HATTON. A 10K gold wedding band found on the middle finger of the left hand is inscribed "Love to W.J.H. from A.J. 9-3-42." All clothing had been removed from this body and was found beside the bodies of Lt. HAYS and Sgt. ADAMS. The apparent discrepancy between the given height and actual table measurement is due to the effects of dehydration with subsequent shrinking of inter-vertebral and other particular cartilage.

2Lt. D. P. Hays
This body is complete, intact and was found lying face up in an extended position. The teeth are in agreement with dental records for 2Lt. HAYS and negative for all other associated crewmembers. A gold wedding band found on the ring finger left hand is inscribed "F.?. to D.H." in agreement with the initials of Lt. HAYS. A gold USAAF Navigator ring with inscription "D. P. HAYS" was found on the middle finger right hand. A bill fold with identification papers for Lt. D. P. HAYS was found in the pocket of the suntan trousers being worn by this crewmember. The estimated height was based upon measurements of two (2) leg bones and is in agreement with the recorded height for 2Lt. D. P. HAYS

SSgt. Samuel E. Adams
This body is complete, intact and was found lying partially on the back and partially on the right side. The teeth are in agreement with dental records of SSgt. ADAMS and negative for all other associated crewmembers. Two (2) identification tags for SAMUEL E. ADAMS were found suspended from the neck on a short length of twine. The chin of this casualty is quite prominent. The estimated height is based upon measurements of the exposed bones of the right arm and the left tibia.

Lt. Robert F. Toner
This body is complete, intact and was found lying on left side with the face covered with sand. The teeth are in agreement with dental records of LT. TONER and negative for the other associated crewmembers. One (1) identification tag for ROBERT F. TONER was found with this remains. Rosary beads and a crucifix recovered with the body is in agreement with the Catholic faith recorded for LT. TONER. Tooth chart comparison could not be made at the site due to the mummified condition of facial area. Two flight jackets were found on the body. The height is based upon an actual table measurement and reflects the results of severe dehydration.

TSgt. Robert E. LaMotte
This body is complete, intact and was found lying on left side with hands drawn up near the face. The teeth are in agreement with dentals records of TSgt. LA MOTTE and negative for the other associated crewmembers. One (1) identification tag for ROBERT E LA MOTTE was found with this remains. Rosary beads and a crucifix recovered with the body are in agreement with the Catholic faith recorded for TSgt. LA MOTTE. The height is based upon an actual table measurement and reflects the results of severe dehydration.

Col. Ben Lambeth and Army captain Myron Fuller read from Lt. Toner's diary.

Chaplain and Lt. Col. William G. Woods reads from the Bible as a solemn service is held for the five crewmen.

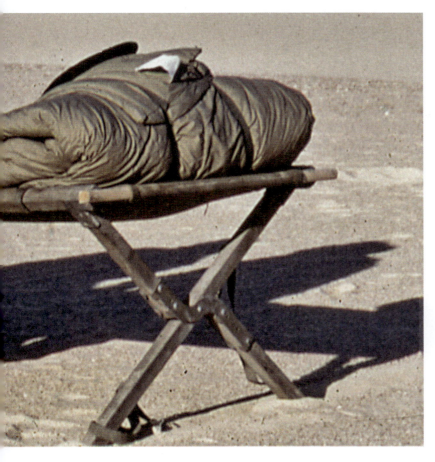

CHAPTER 10 THE DISCOVERY OF FIVE CREW REMAINS

Lt. Toner's diary revealed the suffering the crew went through before their deaths.

Capt. McCash was flight surgeon on the February 1960 recovery of the first five crew remains.

The first five crews remains not long after their discovery.

Investigator Hugo Schaefer walks around the perimeter of the five remains.

Two of the crew's remains. On the left is Lt. Hays, and on the far right, stretched out, is Lt. Hatton.

Recovery crew and investigator Schaefer getting a closer look at the remains.

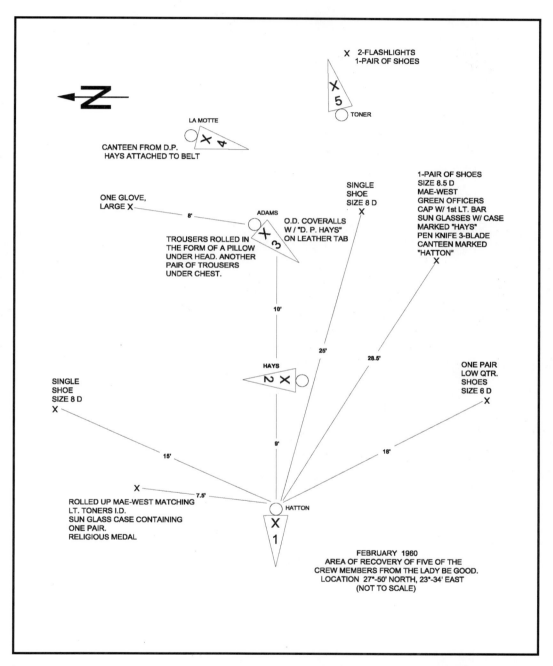

Disposition of the remains of the first five crew members of the Lady Be Good just as they were discovered by the BP oil personnel, February 11, 1960.

Lt. Hatton

Lt. Hatton

Lt. Hatton

Lt. Hatton

Lt. Hatton

The bottom of Lt. Hatton's mummified feet.

Lt. Hays

CHAPTER 10 THE DISCOVERY OF FIVE CREW REMAINS

Lt. Hays

Capt. McCash and Hugo Schaefer start to unearth Lt. Hays.

Lt. Hays

Sgt. Adams

Col. Griffith examining Lt. Toner's remains; note the preservation of the front of the face, which had been covered with sand.

When sand was removed from the back of Lt. Toner's head, it was revealed that his hair was preserved.

The remains of Lt. Toner (*foreground*) and Sgt. LaMotte.

The remains of Sgt. Robert LaMotte.

Remains of the five crew members were covered with their country's flag prior to be carried to the waiting USAF SC-47.

CHAPTER 10 THE DISCOVERY OF FIVE CREW REMAINS

Sun setting on the flag-draped remains of five of the Lady Be Good's crewmen.

Air Force and Army field-investigating personnel recover the five crew members' remains and load them into the aircraft.

Five of the Lady Be Good's crew were finally on their way home, February 1960.

With the recovery complete, USAF personnel head back to their plane and depart back to Wheelus AFB.

Recovery personnel discuss the solemn duty they had just preformed.

CHAPTER 11 ★ SEARCH FOR THE FINAL FOUR: OPERATION CLIMAX

After reading the diary, Fuller and Schaffer now knew that only eight of the crew were together after bailing out. John Woravka, the bombardier, wasn't found that night after landing in the desert. Toner also indicated that engineer Harold Ripslinger, assistant engineer Guy Shelley, and gunner Vernon Moore still had enough strength to walk and had continued on up the valley till they entered the dunes. The IDs of the five men from dog tags and clothing indicated the remains were those of Lts. William Hatton, Robert Toner, and Dp Hays; TSgt. Robert La Motte; and SSgt. Samuel Adams. After the remains were airlifted, first to Wheelus AFB and then on to Frankfurt, Germany, confirmation of positive ID was done by Wes Neep at the identification laboratory.

On the second day at the recovery site, Maj. Rubertus flew a *Life* magazine crew in because of the interest this almost two-year-old story of the Lady Be Good had generated. Later, *Life* published an eight-page article in its March 7, 1960, issue. The article had several photos, including reproductions of the pages from Toner's diary.

With the new evidence obtained from the diary, it was now ascertained that a third search would be necessary to locate the remaining men of the doomed crew. Anything needed to accomplish the mission was supplied by the Departments of the Army and Air Force. Supplied items for the search included six US Army radio-equipped desert-prepped trucks in excellent condition, two almost new US Army Bell H-13 helicopters with spare parts and support crews, a complete field kitchen, a five-man US Army public-information group (including a still photographer and a motion picture photographer), nineteen qualified US Army personnel, and two US Air Force C-130As to transport all these supplies and personnel down to the crash site.

Gen. Spicer had requested and gotten a US Air Force Douglas B-66 reconnaissance aircraft to make a 35,000-foot-high-altitude photoreconnaissance of the next search area to help in locating accessible paths for the trucks through the Sand Sea Dunes. Also, BP gave permission for the full use of their water wells in the region for as long as this large team needed them for the next search area.

In late March, Air Force C-130A aircraft airlifted the search group, helicopters, ground vehicles, and all support equipment to a site called Camp Climax. The camp location was chosen on the edge of the Sand Sea, at the southern tip of a dune finger. The dune projection formed the west side of the valley where the five Lady Be Good crewmen had been found.

An antenna placed at the top of a dune rising above the camp enabled 360-degree communications with search vehicles and the helicopters.

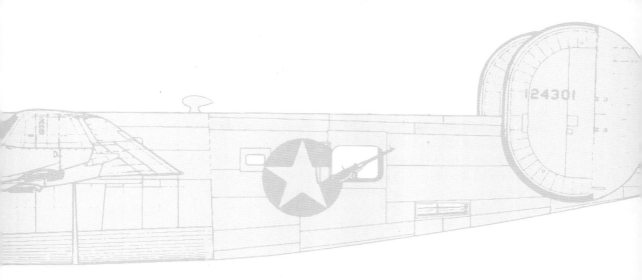

The area to be covered in Operation Climax was a sector extending 50 miles northwest of the five bodies. Three probes to the northwest were made with helicopters sweeping east and west over 10-mile grids. To maintain orientation of the helicopters, trucks were stationed at the eastern and western boundaries of the grids. After the grids had been thoroughly viewed from the air, the truck references were moved forward and the process repeated. As the search moved farther northwest, much time was lost in getting to the search areas and returning to camp. To extend on-site time, a schedule was adopted for search personnel to work double time on alternate days. Off days were utilized to maintain the vehicles and make truck runs to the water well.

On the evening of April 28, 1960, a series of sandstorms started blowing. The first storm subsided around 0900 on the twenty-ninth. A second storm started that night and continued blowing hard until the thirtieth. The nineteen search specialists were made up of people from the US Army's aviation, engineering, signal corps, and mortuary departments looking for the Lady Be Good's crewmen and were scheduled to start this latest search on April 30, using two jeeps with an observer and a driver each. One jeep had Capt. Myron Fuller with driver SPC4 William H. Knight, while the second jeep had SFC Jarvis Wheeler, with PFC Ronald Bingman driving. One jeep was pulling a small trailer with supplies, and both were equipped with mounted compasses for navigation. Early on the thirtieth as the sandstorm abated, Capt. Fuller led the helicopter supply and control vehicles through the dune passage north of Camp Climax, which led to the next valley to the east, where operations were to be conducted. All the trails had been erased by the sandstorm from the night before, which made it quite easy to get lost in the passage.

After leaving red flags showing the route through the dunes, Fuller waited for Wheeler to rendezvous with him, which he did at the eastern end of the passage. They then started their search across the valley, but because another sandstorm started blowing, it made it impossible to see anything within the dunes, so they headed southeast, following the eastern finger of the dunes to pick up a known trail. Fuller radioed Wheeler to follow him, but Fuller had turned southeast alongside the dune finger, keeping it in sight despite the blowing sand, Bingman, driving the second jeep, lagged behind enough to lose sight of Fuller's jeep, then lost Fuller's trail altogether in the blowing sandstorm. Bingman then called on the radio, letting Fuller know he had lost the trail.

Fuller instructed them to turn west back toward the finger of the dune, then follow it south until they came to the tip of the dune, where they would meet them.

Bingman misinterpreted the message as "Go east until you come to a dune finger, then follow it south to the tip and wait for us." Fuller thought he had been talking to Wheeler. Wheeler, thinking there was something wrong with the message he had just been given by Bingman (which there was), took the mike and asked Fuller to repeat the message, but he got no response. By then, communications had broken down because of the sandstorm and the widening distance.

While Wheeler and Bingman were now driving east toward the other side of the valley, looking for the finger of the dune, Fuller and Knight were heading south until they came to the tip of the dune they were following, where they waited. Wheeler and Bingman, on the other hand, kept going east across the valley till they came to the next finger of dunes running south; they then turned south following that set of dunes until they came to the tip, then stopped and waited.

When Wheeler and Bingman didn't show up, Fuller thought that they may have turned southeast earlier than he did, and might be coming southeast on a route farther west. Fuller then drove over a mile and a half west, then northwest, then southeast, and received only snippets of radio blips. Fuller then drove in a huge loop southward across the valley, looking for tracks, but found none; he then returned to Camp Climax, thinking that Wheeler had done the same, but found he had not. Capt. Fuller knew now that they had a big problem.

When Capt. Fuller didn't show up at Wheeler's location, he and Bingman drove another 35 miles southeast, stopped, then drove east and then west, looking for Fuller's jeep tracks; through this entire time, Wheeler attempted to make radio contact, but to no avail. Wheeler kept no mileage, so he had no accurate approximation on his own position, although he thought he did. Because of this, he based all of his subsequent actions on a incorrect location. They kept driving through another line of dunes and thought they was south of Camp Climax; thinking this, they turned around and headed north, thinking he could come back into the valley where a well had been established, and pick up his bearings as well as refilling all their canteens and jerry can. At his farthest point north, they realized they had less than 3 gallons of gas left in the jeep. They felt their only recourse was to drop the trailer and head directly southwest across the dunes, toward what they thought was the valley where the well was.

They spent the night where they left the trailer, then headed out through the dunes the next morning for about 7 miles before the last of the fuel ran out. They stayed at the jeep until May 4, when Wheeler decided to strike out on his own with three canteens of water, thinking he could make it to the next valley, where he thought the well was, and get help. Wheeler walked around 20 miles through the dunes before he gave up and turned back. He had left at 0600 on the fourth, rested that night after 7 miles, then at 0500 on the fifth he continued, crossing three dune fingers and reaching a point east by 1130 on the fifth. He then walked five more miles to a dune and slept from 1630 to 2400. Restarting his walk at midnight, he reached the jeep by 1200 on the sixth, totally exhausted. He started out with three canteens full; on the outbound walk he had consumed two and a half canteens, so all he had coming back was a half canteen, which left him depleted and dehydrated after returning to the jeep.

Back at Camp Climax, the search for the Lady Be Good's crewmen stopped, and attention was concentrated on finding Wheeler and Bingman. After Capt. Fuller's return to camp on the late afternoon of the thirtieth, it was apparent the next step must be taken fast.

Search teams set out that night on the thirtieth, but the sandstorm was still blowing, obliterating any tracks from Wheeler's jeep and trailer. The teams had established light beacons on high dunes, as well as shooting off flares and constantly calling on the radio, but the storm was still going at full force, so by 2400 they packed it in and went back to camp, to resume the search the next morning.

By May 2, the storm had finally subsided to where they could use the Bell H-13 helicopters to help in the search. For the next three days and nights, the search parties kept looking, crisscrossing several different valleys and dune fingers that had been drawn out in a grid on maps. They also called out on the helicopter radio and fired off flares at night but found nothing. Gen. Spicer, head of the 17th Air Force, and Wes Neep flew in to help with the search on the evening of the third. Other aircraft were also called in, flying at higher altitudes on the fourth, including an SC-54 and an SA-16 flying boat.

By May 6, Wheeler and Bingman still hadn't been located, giving Capt. Fuller the idea that the two men may have gone south deep into the gravel plain, possibly trying to reach the Lady Be Good. With this in mind, a plan was devised for May 7–8 to extend the search east and south and to get both the H-13 helicopters ready for a move south to the Lady Be Good.

Wes Neep came up with another idea that Capt. Fuller felt had more merit: that Wheeler and Bingman, in trying to return to camp through what they thought was the passage, may have missed the turn south and passed west into another valley and, through some confusion, had passed farther west. This seemed like a much more plausible direction they may have traveled instead of southeast across the gravel plain, so the search went northward for another 45 minutes of latitude, up to the water well where the gasoline supply vehicles were stationed, then the H-13s flew 5 miles farther north, then to the east, and then started sweeps back north. On their first sweep they found the trailer, then were able to follow the jeep tracks till they found the men; after a full week lost in the Sand Sea of Calanscio, they were both still alive and in fair condition. Wheeler said that they were 18 miles from Camp Climax, when in fact they were more than 50 miles from the camp. The searchers looking for them covered almost 2,500 miles.

On May 12, 1960, a late-afternoon radio message was received that, yet again, a BP oil exploration team had found another airman's remains, 37 miles from the first five bodies. It was later found that the grid search would have reached this same location in two more probes.

The reported location of the sixth remains indicated it would be difficult for the search team's vehicles to make it to the site. After receiving the report, a helicopter was sent out to locate the British team and look for a passage through the dunes for their vehicles.

The helicopter returned to camp after not being able to find the BP team or a passage through the dunes. They weren't even able to establish radio contact with the BP people. A thirteen-man convoy in three vehicles penetrated the dunes on the 305-degree heading. As the convoy proceeded farther into Sand Sea, the heavier trucks bogged down, forcing passages to be sought by the lighter jeep. At the end of the first day, only 26 straight-line miles had been covered, although the circuitous route totaled 55 miles and required frequent use of sand plates. In its constant zigzagging to locate penetrable passages through the dunes, the jeep covered over 120 miles.

Early the next day, a helicopter was sent forward, and the pilot located the British survey party a few miles west of the search group convoy. The scout jeep, guided by the helicopter, rendezvoused with the British party, and searchers learned of the chance discovery of the sixth remains, which occurred during the process of laying out a pipeline route. Providentially, the British party happened upon the body during a lunch break in the dunes.

The remaining search vehicles reached the site after two very difficult hours. The sixth airman had collapsed near the summit of a high dune. The constantly changing shape and motion of the dune surface from the winds had caused dismemberment of the body, which was widely scattered over 250 yards. Portions of the skeletal remains were recovered up to 6 inches below the surface. Deteriorated clothing was found at the foot of the dune. In a trousers pocket, two leather billfolds were found with papers identifying them as the property of TSgt. Harold Ripslinger and SSgt. Guy Shelley Jr. Evidence at the scene tentatively identified the remains as those of Shelley. It was speculated that Ripslinger must have collapsed earlier, southeast of the point Shelley had reached. The presence of both billfolds suggested that after Ripslinger had expired, Shelley took his billfold for forwarding to next of kin.

After two hours of searching, the fifteen members of the group recovered all but 5 percent of the remains of Shelley, as well as two confirming identification tags. It was known that poisonous sand viper snakes inhabited the immediate area, and further probing into the dune entailed serious risk. The remains were returned to Camp Climax.

Air search operations were briefly suspended to perform periodic maintenance on the helicopters. During this interim, Wes Neep revisited the 325-degree trail, originating in the middle of the British Long Range Desert Group 20-degree trail. Questions still remained whether all the airmen had left the well-marked 340-degree trail for the new course. It was possible that one or more of them, walking alone, had continued on the Italian five-track trail into the Sand Sea. The markers left on the 325-degree heading were still in place a year later, when Fuller and Neep attempted to find others that might denote where the crew had left the 340-degree trail. Nothing new was found.

Finally, it was concluded that the three markers oriented in a 325-degree line, found earlier, were actually the starting point of this new trail. While walking on the 325-degree course between the first three markers and the last (barely discernible) parachute arrowhead, Neep found three more pieces of flight equipment, all aligned at 325 degrees. Extending this heading beyond the last parachute marker led to a point 6 miles due east of the dune where Camp Climax was established. Survey flags were placed at this location for guiding a helicopter on a continuation of this course into the Sand Sea.

When the air search was resumed, the helicopters made right-angle sweeps extending for 8 miles on both sides of the 305-degree line between the five crew remains and the site of the sixth airman, 37 miles northwest. By the afternoon of May 17, this search had advanced 26 miles into the dunes. While flying over the east slope of a high dune, helicopter pilot Lt. Joseph Sites, with Wes Neep acting as observer, sighted the barely exposed body of the seventh crew member. A landing was made nearby, and the intact remains of Ripslinger were tentatively identified from a pocket diary and tech sergeant chevrons on a shirt. The gradual slope where the remains were found was relatively stable, and no translation of the body had occurred over the seventeen years. Blowing sand particles had eroded small exposed areas of the skull, right shoulder, and right hip. It appeared from his fetal posture that Ripslinger had expired during the cold of a desert night. The pocket diary, recovered from his shirt pocket, revealed still-legible entries that essentially mirrored those in Lt. Toner's diary. Here is Sgt. Ripslinger's diary in its entirety.

Scheduled to leave Ajes, Maj. Cross postponed until next day.

Left embarkation point 1330, landed Boring Guen, Puerto Bro.

Depart for Atkinson near Georgetown, South America 0815 to 1515. Saw 2 killed in A-20 crash.

Gas not available. Delayed. Field cut out of Jungle.

0635 departed for Natal but landed at Belem due to radio trouble.

Delayed due to gas shortage.

No gas, tanker sunk by sub.

Tanker arrives with 6 million gallons, filled tank in afternoon.

Take off at 0700 but landed due to low fuel pressure. Departed at 0915 and arrived at Natal at 1515.

Departed at 0855 and landed at Ascension Island at 1745.

Departed at 0715. Arrived at Accra, Africa 1600.

50 hour inspection.

Depart at 0840, landed at Maiduguri, Nigeria 1515.

Departed 0655, arrived Kartoum 1530.

1000, departed and landed at Cairo Egypt 1430.

1130 departed for Soluch Libya, landed 1405.

Soluch, spent the night in old bombed out building.

Visited base at Soluch, very heavy rain.

Wet. Now part of 9th Air Force, 514th Squadron, 376th Bomb Group.

Waiting . . . .

First mission to Napels Italy. T.O. at 3:10pm and dropped bombs at 10:00pm. Lost coming back. Bailed out at 2:10am, landed in desert.

All but Warovka met this am, waited a while then started walking. Had 1/2 a sandwich, piece of candy, cap of water in last 36 hours.

Started out early walking & resting. It's now sundown and still going. One teaspoon of water today, rest of the boys are doing fine.

Started early again and walked till about noon. Spent terrible hot afternoon. Started again at 6:pm and walked all night. One spoonful of water is all.

Tired all out. We can hardly walk our 4th day out. A few drops of water each. Can't hold out much longer without aid. Pray.

5th day out and we all thought were gone. All wanted to die during noon it was so hot. Morns. & nites OK. Two drops of water!

Walked all day and night. Suggested Guy, Moore and I make out alone.

Palm Sunday. Still struggling to get out of the dunes & find water.

Believing that the remaining two airmen (Moore and Woravka) would be found in the general area leading up to the latest recovery, searchers went back over the 26 miles of dune ridges between the five remains and Sgt. Ripslinger. There was a high anticipation that SSgt. Vernon Moore would be found along this route. Lt. Toner's diary noted that Moore was considerably weaker than Ripslinger or Shelley and likely would have collapsed before either of his comrades. The dunes were carefully scanned without any further sighting.

The third-phase search ended on May 18. Airlifting the entire group to Wheelus consumed the ensuing three days. In an addendum to their first summary report covering the search for the crew of the Lady Be Good, investigators Wes Neep and Capt. Fuller concluded, "All the areas surrounding the courses followed by still missing 2Lt. John S. Woravka and SSgt. Vernon L. Moore have been thoroughly searched . . . The missing remains are apparently sufficiently covered by sand at this time so as to escape detection."

For the second time, the Lady Be Good was left as a lonely sentinel in a desert inhabited only by transitory oil exploration teams. The only traces of the remaining members of her lost crew were the fluttering parachute markers left in place by the departed search teams. In all, seven recovered airmen were returned to the United States in lieu of being interred in a national cemetery in North Africa. All but Lt. Hays were buried with military honors in their hometowns. Hays's relatives opted to have him interred in a similar ceremony at Arlington National Cemetery.

All evidence suggested that after seventeen years, the case of the Lady Be Good and her crew could be closed at last. But fate had one final card to play.

On August 11, 1960, nearly three months after searchers had departed from Camp Climax, word was received at Wheelus Air Base that yet another human remains had been discovered by a British Petroleum exploration party. The location was just 12 miles northeast of the Lady Be Good crash site. The BP geologists had been traveling across the gravel plain to an oil exploration site south of the B-24 when the airman was spotted.

Since qualified personnel were available at Wheelus to recover the remains, appropriate authorization was forwarded from the Army Quartermaster Mortuary System Headquarters. Maj. Bill Rubertus, by now familiar with the terrain along the route to the Lady Be Good, with copilot Rhea Pinkston and Wheelus director of medical services Col. Edward Cada, met the BP party at the crash site. The Wheelus group was driven immediately to the location of the eighth body, which was lying fully exposed on the gravel surface. The site was barely 2 miles from the northeast limit of the 1959 search by the Army investigators around the B-24 wreckage.

Col. Cada quickly identified the body as that of Lt. John Woravka from dog tags and personal effects. The airman was lying on his back, with the tangled shrouds of a parachute on top of the body, dressed in a complete set of high-altitude clothing.

In a flight coveralls pocket, a well-preserved 3-by-5-inch notebook was found. The pages were blank except for the first, which bore the following hastily scrawled sentence: "He was 'beeching' about something . . . What's going to happen? . . . Are we going home?" These impromptu words were obviously penciled during the final stages of the crew's last flight—presumably during the confused moments leading up to the Lady Be Good turning back over Sorrento, Italy. It was reasonably theorized that Lt. Woravka, seated at his station in the nose of the plane, was attempting to elicit information regarding the course of the mission from navigator Dp Hayes, positioned just to the rear of Woravka. Hayes, ostensibly, was consulted for a heading back to Soluch before Lt. Hatton turned away from Naples.

Fastened to a web belt around Woravka's body was a nearly full canteen of water and a first-aid kit. Col. Cada returned to Wheelus with the canteen and first-aid kit and had laboratory tests conducted on the contents of both items. The water was found to be potable, and the first-aid dressings still sterile after the seventeen years of exposure in the desert. Woravka's failed parachute spared him the drawn-out suffering of the rest of the crew.

The discovery of Woravka finally resolved the issue of whether the other eight crew members had left their well-marked 340-degree trail and ended up on the 325-degree heading. The search team had thought that it was conceivable that Lt. Woravka had been among the first to bail out but had failed to rendezvous with the rest of the crew and had set out singly on the 325-degree heading. It was now clear that all but Woravka had made the decision to leave the marked course along the Italian truck tracks, believing that a heading of 325 degrees would be the shortest path to the coast and their base. After recovering Lt. Woravka's body, the group departed for the short trip to the B-24 crash site. At this time, just four-tenths of a mile southwest of the B-24, the crew rally point after bailing out was discovered. Several sets of high-altitude sheepskin-lined jackets, pants, and boots, as well as Mae West life preservers and fired signal flares, were found. Heavy parachute harnesses had been left in a pile after cutting free the silk parachutes. There was no doubt this was the place the crew had assembled and fired signal flairs for Lt. Woravka before starting their long walk through Hell the next day.

It may have been a good thing the crew was unaware that 458 miles was still lying between them and their base on the Libyan coast, but then again, if they had realized this, it's possible they may have tried to find what was left of their plane, knowing there were several emergency supplies (food, water, etc.) aboard, including the SCR-578 "Gibson Girl" hand-cranked emergency radio that could be tethered to a supplied box kite for an antenna. Two of these were usually carried in the two life raft compartments on the B-24's upper center section.

After Lt. Woravka's discovery, his remains were airlifted to the Frankfurt mortuary for examination. Because he had ended up flat on his back, facing up, the only exposed part of his body was his face, and almost seventeen years of blowing sand, sun, and heat had worn the exposed face down to the skull below the eye sockets, replacing all the soft tissue inside the skull with sand. And because he was fully clothed with his high-altitude flight suit over his uniform, not only was his body mummified, it even retained moisture on the internal organs.

And what became of SSgt. Vernon Moore?

In February 1953, less than ten years after the Lady Be Good failed to return from her first mission, the British 25th Armored Brigade was conducting a training exercise across the Sand Sea of Calanscio from west to east, intersecting the next flat gravel plain on their way to the Kufra Oasis (the same gravel plain that the Lady Be Good and six of her crew had rested on). The unit came across a human skeleton. According to people there at the time, these remains had no identifying clothing of any kind, just the skeleton lying flat on its back, skull face up, and arms outstretched. It looked like the person had died in that position and had never been disturbed. It was impossible to know how long ago this poor soul had perished; it could have been one, ten, or even one hundred years, but at the time, the British thought it was an Arab who had tried to cross the desert. They buried the remains where they were found and moved on. It was speculated decades later, and many years after the discovery of the American bomber and her crew, that the skeleton could have been Vernon Moore. However, considering that these remains had no clothing or identification of any kind and that Moore was with Shelly and Ripslinger when they had entered the dunes—and it was ascertained that the British expedition had entered the Sand Sea south of the point where the three Americans had entered the dunes heading north on their futile attempt to find help—it's a good bet that SSgt. Vernon L. Moore's remains will never be discovered and will be lost forever in the shifting sands of the Calanscio Sand Sea.

At the same time that the Air Force recovered Lt. Woravka's body, they also recovered two of the Lady Be Good's propellers. Led by Air Force lieutenant Ed Heller, his team of mechanics removed the props from engines #1 and #2 and also recovered the last Browning .50-caliber machine gun—which was still attached to the tail turret—to take back to Wheelus Air Base.

In 1962, a US Army truck caravan used the Lady Be Good as a navigational exercise and paid the wreck a visit; photos were taken and are shown here.

Then in 1964, Maj. Bill Rubertus, his wife, and a film representative from the Moody Institute flew out to the crash site in Rubertus's private plane to do an interview with the major on the Lady Be Good story. At that time, structurally, the basic plane was still not in much different condition than it was in 1960.

Between 1965 and 1968, unknown people came to the crash site and did severe damage to the wreck, butchering the fuselage, tail section, nose, and wings. At one point, the entire tail section was hooked to the back of a truck and dragged several yards away from the wing section, tearing off the left vertical stabilizer and a portion of the horizontal stabilizer. Then the forward nose section was torn off the fuselage and crushed by something, possibly the same truck. Sections of the top of the wings had large pieces of the upper wing surface chopped with axes, revealing the interior of the wings. I find it hard to believe why people would want to spend that kind of energy and time destroying this relic in over 130-degree heat.

In 1968, the McDonnell-Douglas Corporation wanted some items off the Lady Be Good for testing to see how they stood up under twenty-five years of exposure to desert conditions. Jim Walker, an aerospace engineer for McDonnell-Douglas, was instrumental in starting the ball rolling on this project. The military also had questions concerning the long-term storage on materials used in combat, so the Society of Automotive Engineers (SAE) arranged for the removal and return of specific hydraulic parts from the Lady Be Good.

The first components were obtained in June 1960, during the final crew search operations and were evaluated at the Air Force's Wright Air Development Division, Wright-Patterson Air Base, in Dayton, Ohio. The results of the tests were shared with several major aerospace corporations, including McDonnell-Douglas. The preservation of these parts after seventeen years of exposure to sun, wind, and blowing sand was remarkable. The McDonnell-Douglas project concerned with long-term missile storage required more components and materials from the Lady Be Good, this time after twenty-five years in the desert. This would give the previous study from 1960 more information concerning corrosion and other data.

The RAF had established an airbase after the war at El Adem, Libya, south of Tobruk. This base was 385 miles due north of the Lady Be Good.

Wing Commander A. V. E. Palmer, who was in charge of the Desert Rescue Team (DRT), was contacted at this base. This unit had the capability to make an overland expedition to the crash site to recover what was needed for testing.

An expedition to the Lady Be Good from El Adem would mean crossing the Sand Sea of Calanscio at the north end, which was 75 miles across.

Flt. Lt. A. P. Zeleny was selected to head the expedition, and Wing Cmdr. Palmer made the decision that the expedition would leave El Adem around mid-April 1968. A list was put together by Jim Walker of McDonnell-Douglas on what components would be selected for removal from the wreck. On April 12, the expedition left El Adem with three Land Rovers and one 3-ton Bedford truck, the latter carrying most of the fuel, water, and spare parts. The route to the Lady Be Good from El Adem was considerably shorter than the more westerly approaches taken by the 1959–60 search teams. The first 150 miles followed a British Petroleum oil pipeline south through scrub desert, before the route entered the Sand Sea. The radio transmission in one Land Rover failed, which caused some problems, but these were overcome. A replacement was brought to the site by a reserve unit of the DRT. The southern edge of the Sand Sea was reached on April 17. The team arrived at the Lady Be Good later the same afternoon and immediately started removing the items listed by Jim Walker.

The DRT team found that the condition of the Lady Be Good had drastically changed since the last official military visit in 1960. The plane had been virtually torn to pieces in the intervening years. Flt. Lt. Zeleny's team took the time to drag the main components of the aircraft back to their perspective original locations. Fortunately, the components and samples they wanted were still there.

The most-important item to be retrieved was one of the engines, which after careful examination was determined to be the #2 engine, still largely intact and complete. A ramp was used that was made from the PSP plates, and the 2,000-pound engine was winched onto the Bedford truck in less than two hours.

When the crash site was first visited in 1959, not one living organism was found near the wreckage. Yet, when the DRT team first arrived at the Lady Be Good, a hawk living inside the fuselage flew off. Later, it became clear that what kept the hawk alive was a large colony of mice, two large lizards, and a weasel that were living in one of the engines, Three swallows orbited overhead all day and appeared to also be living in the aircraft. What appeared to be feeding all of them was the mice, which had stowed away on previous expeditions. The mice in turn lived off the remains of food left by other oil exploration teams that had stopped at the wreck.

All twenty-three items on Jim Walker's list, plus the most important, the engine, were loaded up by April 19. Wing Cmdr. Palmer had flown down from El Adem on the same day with a ration of cold beer for the expedition members, which was greatly appreciated! The expedition departed for El Adem the next morning, on the twentieth, taking the same route back across the Sand Sea that they had come out on.

The DRT Royal Air Force team was the last organized UK/US military visit to the Lady Be Good. In 1969, a military coup in Libya forced King Idris into exile in Egypt. All the US Air Force and Royal Air Force bases were closed in 1971, forced out by Muammar Gaddafi and his nationalist government, who were supported by the Russians. In the intervening years since the British recovered the #2 engine in 1968, not only did more oil exploration teams pay the plane a visit, but several other people also did, doing more damage.

Finally, in August 1994, the remains of the Lady Be Good were recovered by a Libyan team led by a Dr. Fadel Ali Mohamed and deposited in a scrapyard at a Libyan military base on the coast in Tobruk. After 2005, what was left of the plane was moved again and taken to the Gamal Abdul El Nasser Air Base, 10 miles south of Tobruk, and, again, dumped in a storage yard, where it remains to this day. It was

Offloading the two US Army H-13 Bell helicopters that would be used in the search during Operation Climax.

reported in a magazine article that during the recovery in 1994, two guns still remained inside the aircraft "fore and aft," with cannon shells. This was totally incorrect, since (1) B-24Ds never carried "cannon" as armament in 1943 and (2) all ten Browning .50-caliber machine guns this aircraft carried on its first and last mission were recovered by the US Air Force in 1959–60.

A rest period for some of the personnel setting up base camp, known as Camp Climax. Note one of the Army / Air Force personnel getting some sun on the horizontal stabilizer of C-130A, 50014.

As in the first C-130 flight to the crash site back in August 1959, Capt. Shelly McConnell was again involved in flying one of the C-130s that hauled the H-13 helicopters and supplies for Operation Climax.

Lt. Joseph Sites, one of the two Army helicopter pilots used in Operation Climax to look for the final four Lady Be Good crewmen.

Camp Climax being set up as base camp for the search for the rest of the Lady Be Good's crew.

US Army Bell H-13 helicopter being unloaded from a USAF C-130A at the Operation Climax base camp.

Vehicle tracks leading into the Operation Climax base camp, left by trucks and jeeps that had been unloaded from US Air Force C-130As, March 26, 1960.

US Army Bell H-13 helicopters being assembled and made ready to fly the search grids prior to looking for the final four crewmen.

The two H-13s with their observers after landing out in the middle of the desert to go over the search grid map with the search vehicles.

H-13 being refueled by one of the search vehicles that carried extra fuel for the two helicopters.

Three of the US Army search vehicles getting ready to start their search for the two Army enlisted men.

Investigator Wes Neep, 1Lt. Joseph Sites, Capt. Victor Reeves, 1Lt. Robert Judson, and 1Lt. Frank Travino plot out their next move in the search for Lady Be Good's final four crewmen.

CHAPTER 11 SEARCH FOR THE FINAL FOUR: OPERATION CLIMAX

Photo of SFC Jarvis Wheeler taken by 1Lt. Trevino, the pilot of one of the H-13s that found the missing men, May 7, 1960. Note Trevino's and Sites's helicopters on the dune ridge in the background.

SFC Wheeler taking a very long drink as Lt. Trevino gets ready to start his engine and fly Wheeler back to Camp Climax.

PFC Ronald Bingman exiting 1Lt. Sites's helicopter back at Camp Climax after being lost for a harrowing seven days in the Libyan Desert.

PFC Bingman (*left, with cigarette*) and SFC Wheeler (*right, without shirt*) discuss the week they spent in the desert with Capt. Fuller (*with sunglasses*) and other members of Operation Climax, May 7, 1960.

Wes Neep meets Don Livingston from the BP Oil survey crew, who had just discovered the remains of the sixth crew member, Sgt. Guy Shelley.

SSgt. Guy Shelley's remains, as found scattered across the face of a dune.

SSgt. Guy Shelley's foot still encased within his shoe, with his tibia and fibula still attached.

Recovery team reassembles SSgt. Guy Shelley's bones after sifting through the side of the dune from the top to the bottom.

Investigator Wes Neep takes stock of the small amount of clothing that was also recovered from the steep dune.

Sgt. Harold Ripslinger

Three members of the recovery team stand near Sgt. Ripslinger's partially exposed remains, as found.

The remains of Sgt. Ripslinger, exposed to the blowing sand and sun for over seventeen years.

Head-to-foot view of Sgt. Ripslinger, as discovered.

Foot-to-head view of Sgt. Ripslinger, as discovered.

Exhumation and recovery of Sgt. Ripslinger's remains.

After placing Ripslinger's remains on a body bag, the recovery team continues to look for anything else that may belong.

Ripslinger's remains after being placed on the body bag; note that his left forearm and hand had become detached when he was moved.

A small service is preformed by the recovery team at the site as the American flag is placed around the remains.

Sgt. Shelley and Sgt. Ripslinger are saluted; back together again after seventeen years.

The two Lady Be Good crewmen await their journey back home.

The two caskets are loaded aboard a C-130 for the flight back to Germany.

CHAPTER 11 SEARCH FOR THE FINAL FOUR: OPERATION CLIMAX

Lt. John Woravka's remains, as found. He died where he landed after he bailed out and his parachute did not deploy properly.

Lt. John Woravka's body was well preserved other than what was openly exposed to blowing sand and sun for seventeen years.

Rally point where the crew met up the night they bailed out. Scattered around were their Mae West life preservers, parachute shroud lines, high-altitude flight boots, and other assorted items.

"Gibson Girl" hand-cranked emergency radio.

Operating instructions for the "Gibson Girl."

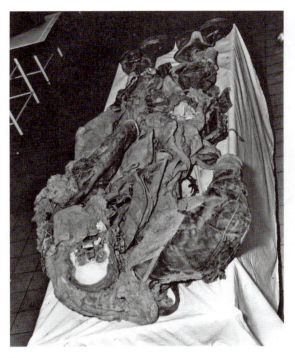
Lt. Woravka's body after being returned to Germany for examination.

Another view of Woravka's body on the examination table.

Sand dunes of the Sand Sea of Calanscio.

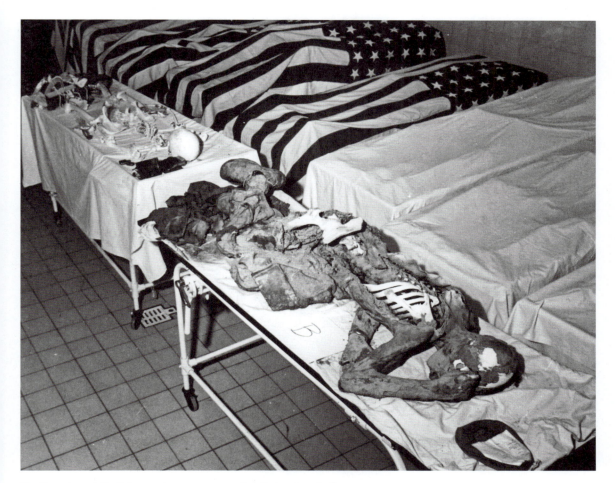
Ripslinger's and Shelly's remains on gurneys after their return to Germany.

Trackless towering dunes in the San Sea of Calanscio where Sgt. Shelly's remains were found.

CHAPTER 11 SEARCH FOR THE FINAL FOUR: OPERATION CLIMAX

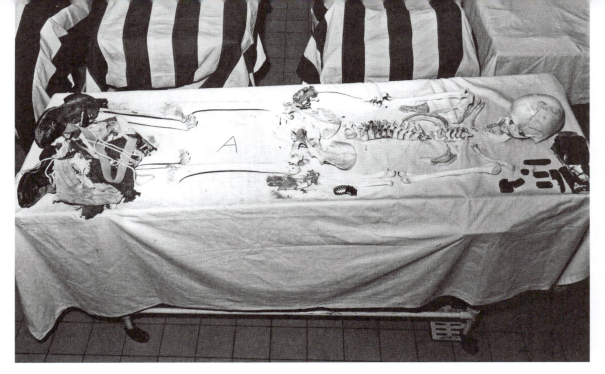

All of Sgt. Shelly's bones recovered from the side of the steep dune. About 90 percent were recovered.

View of the Lady Be Good taken on an overcast day.

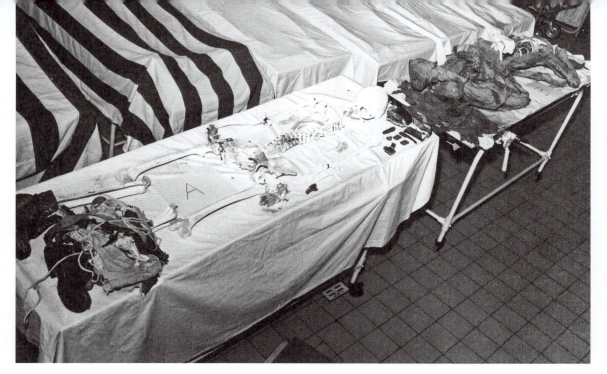
Another view of Shelly and Ripslinger.

CHAPTER 11 SEARCH FOR THE FINAL FOUR: OPERATION CLIMAX

Another view of Lady Be Good on a rare overcast day.

Lt. Ed Heller stands next to the #2 engine. He and his crew flew down to the crash site to remove and bring back the props from the #2 and #3 engines, August 1960.

USAF mechanics in the process of removing both #2 and #3 propellers from the Lady Be Good.

Heller's crew removing the #1 and #2 props from Lady Be Good and loading them into their USAF SC-47.

Close-up of the propeller hub removed by Heller's team.

September 1960: a lot of changes to Lady Be Good since the first photos taken by the USAF in May 1959.

Parts to the plane from the 1943 crash still scattered out in front of the nose.

Lt. Heller (*left*) and his team disassembling Lady Be Good's propellers. It was getting rather warm around this time—noon in August.

Treasure hunters and vandalism have started to take their toll on the B-24.

A 1962 photo taken by a US Army truck caravan that stopped at Lady Be Good.

PFC Roger Landry beside the letters "Good," Lady Be Good crash site, 1962.

Landry (*standing on Lady Be Good's side*) and US Army personnel inspect the interior. Note that the #4 engine has been flipped over and now faces up.

Landry leaning on Lady Be Good's right main landing gear, 1962.

Maj. Bill Rubertus, his wife, and a film representative from the Moody Institute land near Lady Be Good for a film shoot, 1964.

Film interview with Maj. Rubertus by a representative from the Moody Institute, 1964.

Between 1965 and 1968, a severe amount of damage was done to Lady Be Good by unknown people.

Jim Walker posing next to the Lady Be Good's #2 engine in St. Louis, 1968.

Royal Air Force Desert Rescue Team (DRT) ready to winch the Lady Be Good's #2 engine, complete with cowling, onto a flatbed truck.

With the ramp secured, the engine is pulled up onto the truck with chains.

The RAF's DRT team poses with the secured Pratt & Whitney R-1830 engine for the long journey to St. Louis, Missouri.

Flt. Lt. Zeleny, leader of the Long Range Desert Rescue Team, poses for one last photo in front of what was left of Lady Be Good's nose.

Jay Howard's team inspecting Lady Be Good in late 1968. The detached #3 engine was rolled over in front of the #4 engine firewall, while what was left of the #4 engine was dragged from the other side of the aircraft and set in front of the #3 engine mount.

Another 1968 Jay Howard image, showing the deterioration of the aircraft as it was slowly hacked to pieces.

This photo shows how the desert pink overpaint is getting naturally sand-blasted off, revealing the factory olive drab paint beneath.

Still showing most of its desert pink paint, Lady Be Good's vertical stabilizer had been somewhat protected from the sandblasting.

Another group of images taken by Jay Howard; however, four years later, in 1972. By this time, vandals in the intervening years had chopped into what was left of the plane with axes.

The crushed and torn-off nose section has almost no resemblance to its former self.

By 1972, pretty much all the desert pink paint was gone.

Pulverized and crushed, the B-24 flight deck was just a mass of twisted metal.

The American white star and the wind deflector were still visible in 1972 on the left side of the aft fuselage, which shows almost no desert pink left.

A few slivers of Plexiglass still remained wedged in the remnants of the cockpit framing.

Michael Savvides's photos, taken in 1977, show just how much sand had accumulated around the wreck.

Looking from the remnants of the dorsal turret out toward the right wingtip, 1977.

Most of the tail turret components were still there in 1977.

After being brought out of the desert in 1994 by the Libyan government, what was left of Lady Be Good was dumped into a storage yard on the coast in Tobruk. It was a twisted jumble and no longer resembled an aircraft.

Lady Be Good's #3 engine in the dirt in front of one of the engine mounts, 1994.

Lady Be Good's vertical stabilizer, showing her serial number in yellow painted on the olive drab paint from the factory in San Diego, California.

Considerably more damage was done to what was left of the B-24 when it was loaded in four separated pieces, transported, and later dumped off.

Exposed belly and left side of the remains of the back half of the fuselage.

Crushed cockpit section shoved up against the back fuselage.

The gutted remains of a once-proud World War II US Army Air Force four-engine bomber lies in a twisted heap near the coast of Libya, at the Gamal Abdel El Nasser Air Base, south of Tobruk. The Lady Be Good should have been left where she crashed in the desert.

CHAPTER 12 ★ MYSTERIES AND THE SO-CALLED CURSE OF THE LADY BE GOOD

The disassembly and inspection of the #2 engine by the engineers from McDonnell-Douglas, led by Jim Walker, found that fine particles of sand had coated all the moving internal parts of the engine. All of it was from the short time the Lady Be Good spent with the 376th Bomb Group in 1943; this would account for all the aborts from engine troubles on the squadron's combat missions flying from their base in Libya. But what was also found in the rocker cover on the #1 cylinder of the #2 engine was a punched-in hole through one of the rocker arm boxes. What Jim Walker found inside was a piece of a 20 mm cannon shell fired from a German night fighter. Because of this attack sometime after the Lady Be Good left the target area in the dark, it's unknown when or even if the #2 engine was shut down; the damage from this was so slight that the engine probably didn't show any problems. It was originally thought it was shut down when it ran out of fuel deep into the Libyan Desert. Unfortunately, there was no mention of this attack in either Toner's or Ripslinger's diaries, so it's possible the crew had no idea that there was an attack.

And then there's the "Curse" associated with the Lady Be Good. This has to do with items that were removed from the wreck and installed on other aircraft. The first involved the radio from the Lady Be Good, which was removed from the aircraft and used to replace the one that had malfunctioned in the first USAF SC-47 flown down to the crash site on May 25, 1959. There's quite a story behind this. The story starts just two weeks after the SC-47 returned from the southern Libyan Desert.

At 0630, Saturday morning, June 7, 1959, Airman Don Poirier reported to the flight line at Wheelus Air Force Base, Benghazi, Libya, for a 0730 takeoff for Bitburg, Germany, as aircraft radio operator.

The mission was a turnaround to pick up a load of 20 mm aerial cannons along with other supplies for the fighter contingent at Wheelus, with no layover, just fuel stops.

Seven people boarded USAF Douglas SC-47, #0-3689, for the flight to Germany. At this time, the crew consisted of Maj. Smith as pilot, a first lieutenant as copilot, a captain as navigator, crew chief Sgt. "Willy" Williams, and radio operator Airman Don Poirier. Passengers were 1Lt. White and Sgt. James Parker, Poirier's NCOIC. The plan was to pick up Capt. Guy Alphin in Germany because of his night instrument rating, needed for the return flight to Libya. Capt. Alphin was based at Wheelus and had a wife and newborn baby waiting for him there.

The takeoff and the flight across the Mediterranean Sea were uneventful, with a good tail wind pushing them along. But the weather over the European continent was fast deteriorating.

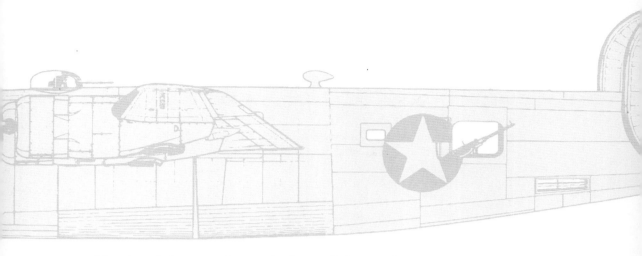

The aircraft they were flying in had a small claim to fame, since this was the very same SC-47 that just two weeks before had brought the first US Air Force investigation team over 400 miles deep into the Libyan Desert to land at the crash site of the Lady Be Good.

On that May 25, 1959, flight down to probably THE most inhospitable, desolate place on the face of the earth, 689's radio ceased to function, which created a big problem. After landing at the Lady Be Good's crash site, the crew were supposed to contact Wheelus AFB on the coast to let them know of their safe arrival. If the Air Force didn't receive this call, they were to launch a rescue operation.

After their safe landing at the crash site, it was discovered that the Lady Be Good's radio, a BC-348 HF radio receiver/transmitter, was exactly the same as the C-47's, and that it still worked perfectly after sixteen years in the searing 135-degree heat. The receiver was removed from the B-24 and installed in 689, just in time to contact Wheelus and stop the rescue mission, which was in the process of being put together.

This same radio was still in 689 as she flew into the gathering storm clouds and darkness toward Germany. On arrival at the US Air Force base in Bitburg, the 20 mm cannons, crated in boxes, were loaded and Capt. Alphin took over as first pilot. After a quick bite to eat for passengers and crew, the heavily loaded C-47 took off for her next stop for more supplies and fuel at Rammstein, Germany.

A storm had developed over southern Europe, with massive thunderheads, lightning, and rain. Before departing Bitburg, they had added one more passenger, an Army enlisted man for the flight back, but Poirier suggested that, considering the heavy load and the storm, the soldier might think about staying behind at Rammstein till the next flight; considering this, the enlisted man put his bag over his shoulder and climbed out of the plane at Rammstein just before 689's takeoff for her last fuel stop at Marseilles, France. This later turned out to be a wise move on his part.

By 2300, they had departed Marseilles, flying into the teeth of the storm. The tail wind, which had helped them along on the flight out, was now a 75-knot headwind, causing major fuel consumption as the plane was buffeted by lightning, rain, and winds. There was talk among the crew to detour to the island of Malta until the storm had passed over the Mediterranean, but Capt. Alphin said that he felt they could make it all the way to the North African coast. He also very much wanted to get back to Wheelus to be with his wife and baby. Things rapidly worsened to the point where Capt. Alphin asked Poirier to call Wheelus to find out if there were better winds at a lower altitude.

Wheelus answered back and told them to descend to between 8,000 and 3,000 feet. Dropping below 11,000 feet, Capt. Alphin, after noting the alarming fuel consumption, decided to shut down the #2 engine on the decent to conserve fuel. This was against the suggestion from Sgt. Williams, the crew chief, who indicated he thought this wasn't a good idea, considering the adverse weather conditions. All this time, brilliant lightning flashes lit up the black storm clouds as winds and lashing rain pummeled the aircraft.

As 689 approached the 5,000-foot mark, Capt. Alphin attempted to restart the #2 engine, but to no avail. With very little power, the plane continued to descend, and at 3,000 feet Capt. Alphin ordered Poirier to send out a "Mayday" and to get Sgt. Williams up front to help him restart the #2 engine—they were in trouble.

689 was now well below 3,000 feet and making only 60 indicated knots while still dropping, with only the #1 engine running at full power. Alphin gave the order to immediately jettison the cargo. Poirier and everyone else started to drag the crates of 20 mm cannon over to the cargo door and dump them out. As Poirier lifted one end to flip it out the open door, Sgt. Williams yelled "Don't flip it; push it out or it'll hit the tail!" He did this, and a split second after shoving the crate out, he heard it hit the water in the inky blackness; they were VERY low! To make matters worse, the #1 propeller started a high-pitched whine, indicating that it was starting to run away. The "brace for crash" bell sounded at that moment, giving Poirier seconds to grab something and hang on. They hit the crest of a wave with a loud bang and bounced to the next wave, settling with a crash. Sgt. Williams was launched like a bullet through the fuselage, impacting the forward bulkhead. Dirt and debris from the floor, along with the rest of the cargo, were thrown everywhere, hitting the people in the fuselage. Poirier was hit in the head with a tie-down ring, causing a gash above the eyebrow.

After 689 settled into the water, Don climbed back up to the rear bulkhead to try to remove the "Gibson Girl" emergency transmitter radio. In spite of all his efforts, he couldn't get it unfastened from its frozen clamps.

The waves were massive, with at least 60-foot troughs causing the C-47 to ride up the face of one wave with her nose pointing high up at a 45-degree angle, then ride over the crest and slide down the other side, burying the nose and engines deep into the wave at the bottom of the trough, causing the tail to lift high out of the water.

Considering that the plane stayed in one piece and with almost empty fuel tanks, the C-47 floated quite well. The time of impact was approximately 0515, with the gray dawn filtering through the rain and gray sky. They were 61 miles short of their destination.

Unbeknown to the people in the rear of the plane, the runaway #1 propeller had come apart on impact with the wave, breaking the blades off and slicing through the left side of the nose just behind the cockpit windows. Capt. Alphin was hit by one of these blades, slicing into his head just behind the ear and splitting his side open from the bottom of his rib cage down through his thigh to his kneecap. The force had shoved his seat up under the center console, trapping his legs.

Back in the tail, Poirier and Sgt. Williams, who had somewhat recovered from his impact with the forward bulkhead, were both furiously trying to release the five-man life raft from the rear bulkhead. It finally broke loose, but not before the lanyard to release the CO_2 to inflate it was accidentally yanked, starting the inflation process inside the plane! Williams forcibly kicked the raft out of the cargo door before it was fully inflated. He followed the raft out and just barley landed in one end. Don followed but missed and ended up on the face of a wave, with his left hand holding on to the inboard trailing edge of the left wing root and his right hand holding on to a line on the raft.

This created a problem for Poirier. As the plane slid down the face of one wave, the trailing edge of the wing, which Don was holding on to, would rise out of the water, creating a space under the wing. As 689 started up the other side of the wave, the tail and wings would smack back down, with Poirier under the trailing edge of the inboard flap, hitting him on the head and putting him underwater each time this happened. He finally extracted himself from this predicament and climbed into the raft.

The two men pulled the raft back over to the open cargo door to help the people still in the plane get into the raft. Maj. Smith yelled out that Capt. Alphin was trapped in the cockpit and needed help, so Sgt. Williams jumped back in the fuselage to lend a hand while Poirier helped the rest of the passengers into the raft.

The extraction of Capt. Alphin was difficult. They had to cut all his clothes off below the waist and pry some of the twisted metal from around his seat; he was in very bad shape, bleeding from massive open wounds.

Back in the raft, the bitter cold and salt spray made it difficult to inflate their Mae West life vests. Poirier went from one person to the other, helping to get this accomplished. Hearing an increasing roar over the wind, the men in the raft looked up to see a USAF Search & Rescue SA-16 Albatross amphibian fly directly over the bobbing C-47 and keep going; they never saw the plane or raft.

By this time, the rescue operation was in full progress. There had been a big party at the base at Wheelus the night before. Many of the flight crew were sleeping in with hangovers, but when the "Mayday" call came in before 0500, several of the pilots volunteered to fly out into the storm to find their friends. One SC-47 took off. With the location given by Poirier on the Lady Be Good's transmitter, the rescue C-47 flew directly to the ditching spot, wagging their wings back and forth and circling the downed plane and raft. The Navy also sent a Lockheed P-2V Neptune out from Naples, Italy, to direct operations from higher up.

As the C-47 from Wheelus circled, a C-54 arrived on scene and pushed out a five-man raft with survival gear. This was a welcome sight to the men in the water, because earlier, as their raft was pushed out of 689's open door, it had caught on something that punctured the side, causing it to start deflating.

The raft pushed out of the C-54 inflated on the way down and hit the water 100 feet from the men. These rescue rafts came with a sea anchor attached to a line on one end of the raft. The sea anchor would act as a pivot point, catching the top of a 60-foot wave and spinning the raft like a top at the end of the line out over the trough, until the centrifugal force flung the whole assembly over to another wave farther away, until the raft disappeared. This was repeated with four more rafts, with the same result, until the C-54 had none left and gave up.

Maj. Smith and one other man had put Capt. Alphin in the raft and, after everyone was secured, asked Poirier to help comfort him, knowing the two were friends. Poirier cradled the injured man's head in his lap, holding and talking to him, but he could see that the captain wasn't going to make it. The floor of the raft was now slippery with Alphin's intestines, and Poirier could see an open gash in his head, exposing portions of his brain.

Guy Alphin died a short time later, and after a brief silence and because of the condition of the sinking raft, they slipped the lifeless body over the side and watched it sink beneath the cold, green waves.

While all this was going on, the raft was deflating and filling with water from the ice-cold spray and waves. It was decided that several of the crew would get out of the raft and hang on to the ropes on the side to keep it from sinking. As they hung on to the raft's sides, they watched old 689 drift off, still afloat and in one piece, visible for almost three hours until she disappeared behind the huge waves.

Rocker arm cover and valve from the #2 engine, showing damage from a 20 mm cannon shell entering after an attack from a German night fighter on the April 4, 1943, mission. This was discovered by Jim Walker during his disassembly of the engine in 1968.

Douglas SC-47, 0-3689, refueling at one of the oil camps on its way down to the Lady Be Good crash site.

Tony John and William C. Riley next to the ill-fated de Havilland U1-A Otter.

After almost four hours in the water, a USAF Sikorsky H-19 rescue helicopter appeared overhead and dropped a note, telling the men in the raft that they were going to lower a rescue basket to haul them up, one at a time.

The captain, acting as navigator, who had attempted to swim out to try to snag one of the rafts dropped by the C-54, was the first to be picked up.

As the H-19 came back over the raft to pick up the rest of the crew, waves were slapping the bottom of the fuselage, causing the helicopter to pull up abruptly to avoid getting swamped. This was repeated several times until they were able to extract the rest of the raft's occupants, with Maj. Smith and Poirier being the last two to be winched aboard. After four and a half hours in the ice-cold water, they were finally heading home.

The H-19 was fast running out of fuel, prompting the flight crew to make a direct-line flight to a small resort village on the coast of Libya called Zabratha, landing on the beach with just fumes left in the tanks.

Hours later, ambulances arrived from Wheelus Air Base, 45 miles away, to take them back to the hospital. Thus ended their harrowing experience, but not without a loss—the young pilot who just wanted to get home that night to be with his wife and baby.

689 sank 61 miles off the Libyan coast in what's probably one of the deepest portions of the Mediterranean Sea, at around 2,000 feet in depth. She sank in one piece and is still down there to this day—with Lady Be Good's HF radio receiver still in place.

And then there was one of the armrests from the Lady Be Good, which was removed from the bomber and was later, because it was deemed more comfortable, installed on a US Army de Havilland U1-A Otter, serial number 0-76115, used by the US Army Geodetic Detachment at Benina Airport, Benghazi. Like the SC-47, in January 1960, while on a flight from Benghazi to Tripoli, it crashed into the Gulf of Sirte. Ten crew were killed and their bodies were never recovered. Only a few items from the plane washed up onshore afterward, the armrest from the Lady Be Good being one of them.

...

A 17-foot-high stained-glass window was commissioned and paid for by US Air Force personnel at Wheelus AFB in 1959–60, as a memorial to the Lady Be Good's crew. The jewellike glass was created by famed German artist Peter Hess and installed at the Wheelus Air Force Base chapel. The base was closed in 1971 after Libya's takeover by Muammar Gaddafi in September 1969. The window was then disassembled and transported to the US Air Force Museum in Dayton, Ohio, where it remains on display to this day (see page 254).

This 17-foot-high stained-glass window was commissioned and paid for by US Air Force personnel at Wheelus AFB in 1959–60, as a memorial to the Lady Be Good's crew. The jewellike glass was done by famed German artist Peter Hess and was installed in the Wheelus Air Force Base chapel.

IN MEMORY OF NINE WHO MADE THE DESERT A HIGHWAY FOR OUR GOD
ANNO DOMINI 1943

LORD GUARD AND GUIDE THE MEN WHO FLY

INDEX

Accra, West Africa, 18, 38
Adams, Samuel, 37, 40, 58, 164–167, 181
ADF, 17–18, 49
Alamogordo Army Air Base, 36
American Graves Registration, 49
Appold, Norm, Col., 18–19, 25, 162
Arnold, Casey, 9
Arnold, Jay, 9
Ascension Island, 17

Backhaus, James, 162
Belem, Brazil, 17, 38
Benghazi, Libya, 46, 48, 63, 90, 133–134, 137, 162, 248
Benina, 48, 253
Berka 2, 18, 50, 134–135
Bingman, Ronald PFC, 189–191, 213
Bin Ramadan, Sayid, 62, 74
Blenheim, bomber, 60–61, 66–69
Blockhouse Rock, 64–65, 74
Bomb Group, 376th, 18, 38, 162
Bomb Squadron, 514th, 18, 38, 49, 62
Borenquen Field, Puerto Rico, 38
Bowerman, Gordon, BP oil, 60–64
British Petroleum (BP), 60, 162–163, 188, 190, 194, 197
Britt, Lt., 47

Cada, Edward, Col., flight surgeon, 194–195
Cairo, Egypt, 18, 38, 91
Calanscio, Sand Sea, 60–61, 130–131, 134, 137, 161–162, 164, 188, 190, 192, 195–197
Climax, Operation, 188–190, 192, 194, 201–204
Compton, Keith Col., 18
Consolidated Aircraft Corp., 10, 12
Costello, Robert, CBS Film, 162

D'Arcy Exp. Co., 60, 62, 64–65, 91
Desert Rescue Team, (DRT), 197, 238–239

Dolezal, Oldrich, Silver City pilot, 162

Elder, Henry, Col., 80–81, 86, 102

Fadel, Ali Mohamed Dr., 198
Fallon, Paul, Col., 47, 162
Feeley, Ed, Lt., 46–48
Flavelle, Brian Lt., 51
Fogel, Ernest, Lt., 51
Fort Worth, Texas, 10, 13
Fuller, Myron, Capt., 64–65, 76, 81–82, 90, 102, 130–131, 133, 135, 137, 141–143, 155, 163–164, 168, 188–191, 194, 213

Gamel Abdul El Nassar Air Base, 198
G.I. Gennie, 25
Gluck, Lt., 46, 48
Gochner, Tom, Lt., 161
Grace, Ralph, Lt., 16, 24–25
Griffith, Stebbins, Col., 162–163, 181

Hatton, 36–43, 46-49, 54–55, 62, 130, 132, 134, 136, 159, 162, 164–166, 173, 176–179, 188, 195
Hays, DP, 36, 38, 40, 44, 54, 62, 91, 165–166, 173, 179–181, 188, 194–195
Hays, Harry, Maj., 64a–65
Heliopolis Airport, Cairo, 18, 38
Heller, Ed, Lt., 196, 230–231
Hellewell, Charles, pilot, 60
Hodne, Gilbert, PFC, 80, 87, 89, 94
Hoover, Roscoe, Sgt., Rose crew, 16
Howard, Jay, 240–244

Iovine, Guy, Lt., 51
Iverson, K. P. Lt., 48, 51

John, Tony, 252

Kesler, Millard Lt., Rose crew, 16, 22–24
Knight, William, SPC4, 189
Kolbus, Walt, Col., 63–64

Kufra Oasis, 60, 61, 63, 130, 132, 195

Lady Be Good, name, 16, 109
Lambeth, Ben, Col., 164, 168
La Motte, Robert, Sgt., 37, 40, 91–92, 164–167, 182, 188
Landry, Roger, PFC, 234–235
Lavin, Maj., 47
Lear, Dean, Lt., 48
Leavy, Allyn, Sgt., Rose crew, 16
Livingstone, Don, BP oil, 214
Long Range Desert Group, 66–69, 132, 192, 239

Maeski, Joe, Pvt., Rose crew, 16
Malta, Island, 19, 47–48
Marr, Griffen, Lt., 80, 81, 90, 121
Marshall, Chuck, Sgt., Rose crew, 16
Martin, John D'Arcy, 60, 62–64
McCain, Lt., 38, 48–49
McCash, Paul, Capt., flight surgeon, 170
McClean, Ronald, D'Arcy, 60–61
McConnel, Sheldon, Capt., USAF, 134–136, 152, 202
McDonnell-Douglas Aircraft, 196–197, 248
Meadote, James, A1C, 80, 92, 121, 123
Midgley, Charles, Lt., 16, 22–24
Moore, Vernon, Sgt., 37, 40, 44, 58, 132, 164, 188, 194–196
Morrison Field, 17, 37, 164

9th Air Force, 38
Naples, Harbor, 19, 39, 46, 91, 195
Natal, Brazil, 17, 38
Neep, Wesley, 64, 76, 80, 90, 92, 94, 100, 122, 124, 130, 133, 135, 137, 147, 164, 188, 191–192, 194, 210, 214–215
Nelson, Lt., 16, 19, 24

Palermo, Sicily, 38
Palmer, VE, wing commander, 197
Paule, James, Capt. (Dr.), 57, 81, 92, 110–111, 123
Pinkston, Rhea, Capt., 80, 102, 194
Poirier, Don, 248–251
Post, John, Capt., 80, 92

Quartermaster mortuary, 64, 194

RAF, 18, 57, 60, 197
Rafeld, Russell, A1C, 80, 90, 121–122

Ripslinger, Harold, Sgt., 36–38, 40, 54, 164, 192, 194, 196, 216–220, 225, 227
Rose, Dawson, Lt., 16–22, 24, 39
Rubertus, Bill, Maj., 80, 86, 90, 94, 96, 98, 100, 134–135, 162–163, 188, 196, 236

Saly & Co. Ltd. 130, 135, 143, 147
Savvides, Michael, BP oil, 244, 245
Schaeffer, Hugo, 164, 171, 174, 188
Senussi, Mohammed, Kufra P. D., 63
Shea, Sgt., 62
Shelly, Guy, Sgt., 37, 40, 58, 188, 192, 194, 196, 214–216, 221, 225–227
Sheridan, Don, 60, 62–64
Silver City Air, 162
Simmons, Hal, Capt., 18, 39, 49
Sites, Joseph, 192, 202–213
Soluch, Libya, 18, 25, 33, 38, 46–48, 91
Soukup, Lt., 47
Spicer, Gen., 133, 141–142, 188, 191
Swarner, Lt., 46, 48

39th Troop Carrier Squadron, 134
Thompson, Harry, Lt. Col., 135–136, 155
Toner, Robert, Lt., 36, 38, 40, 43, 46, 54, 58, 62, 126, 164–167, 181–182, 188
Topeka, Kansas, 16, 37–38
Travino, Frank, Lt., 210, 212
Tripoli, Libya, 64, 133
Truthson, Ed, 9

Valentine, Carl, Pvt., Rose crew, 16
Venturini, Don, Army, 125

Walker, James, 196–197, 237, 248–253
Waller Army Air Base, 17
Walsh, Capt., 47–48
Wheeler, Jarvis SFC, 189–191, 212
Wheelus AFB, 57, 63–65, 80, 90, 130, 133–134, 137, 162, 164, 185, 194–195
Wiesbaden, Germany, 63, 130
Woods, Wayne, Sgt., 80, 102
Woods, William, chaplain, 163, 169
Woravaka, John, 36, 38, 40, 44, 55, 62, 91, 164, 188, 194–195, 196, 222, 224–225
Worley, Lt., 48
Wright, F. C., Lt., 47

Zeleny, 197, 239